# knitted woodland creatures

A collection of cute critters to make

Susie Johns

THE GUILD OF MASTER CRAFTSMAN
PUBLICATIONS

First published 2014 by
Guild of Master Craftsman Publications Ltd
Castle Place, 166 High Street, Lewes,
East Sussex BN7 1XU

ISBN 978-1-86108-917-5

The publishers and author can accept no legal responsibility for any
consequences arising from the application of information, advice or
instructions given in this publication.

A catalogue record for this book is available from the British Library.

Publisher  Jonathan Bailey
Production Manager  Jim Bulley
Managing Editor  Gerrie Purcell
Senior Project Editor  Sara Harper
Copy Editor  Cath Senker
Managing Art Editor  Gilda Pacitti
Art Editor  Rebecca Mothersole
Designer  Ginny Zeal
Photographer  Andrew Perris

Set in Frutiger
Colour origination by GMC Reprographics
Printed and bound in China

**For my children Josh, Lillie and Edith,
who share my love of animals, both knitted and real,
and who are a constant support and inspiration.**

# Where those creatures hide

# Introduction

When you go for a walk in the woods, you may be fortunate enough to catch a glimpse of a rabbit or a squirrel – but most of the creatures that live there prefer to remain hidden from humans. So this book offers you the chance to make your own woodland companions, using needles and yarn.

Most of the patterns are designed for those with some knitting experience, but inexperienced knitters should not be deterred, although knitting toys requires a slightly different approach from making jumpers or scarves. Knitting novices are advised to begin with the Chipmunk, the Raccoon or the Frog, each of which is composed of pieces knitted flat using the two-needle method. Knitting the pieces for these creatures is straightforward, as long as you follow the pattern carefully. The bigger challenge comes when you join the pieces together, which will require you to stitch a neat seam and shape the finished creature.

Making these woodland creatures isn't just about knitting the component parts: it is about constructing them and giving each one a personality. Read through the pattern instructions before you begin, to make sure you understand what skills are required, and check out the techniques section at the back of the book.

I have thoroughly enjoyed creating the patterns for these creatures, seeing them take shape and develop their own individual 'personalities', and I hope you will have as much fun making them.

Susie Johns

MOLE >> 58

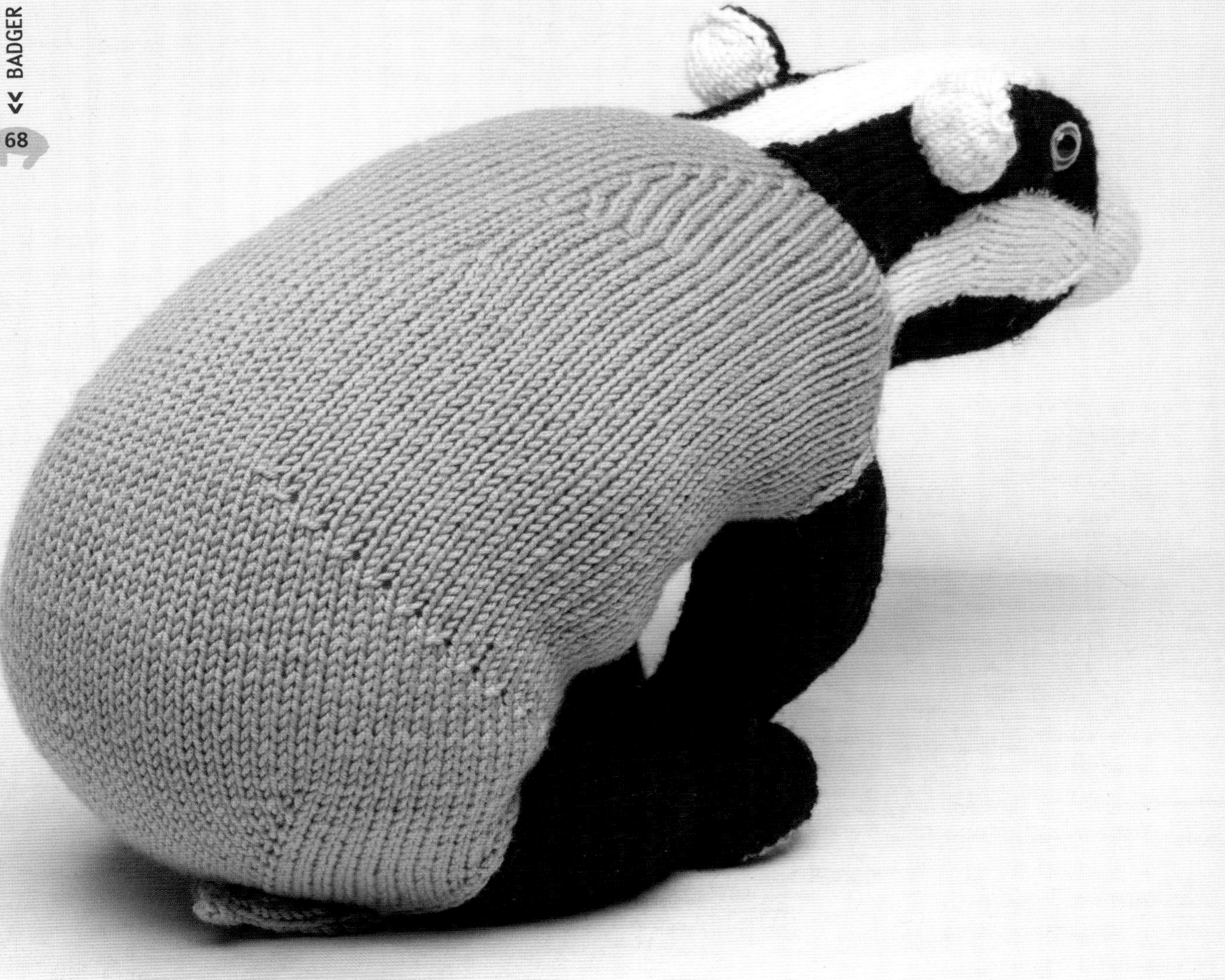

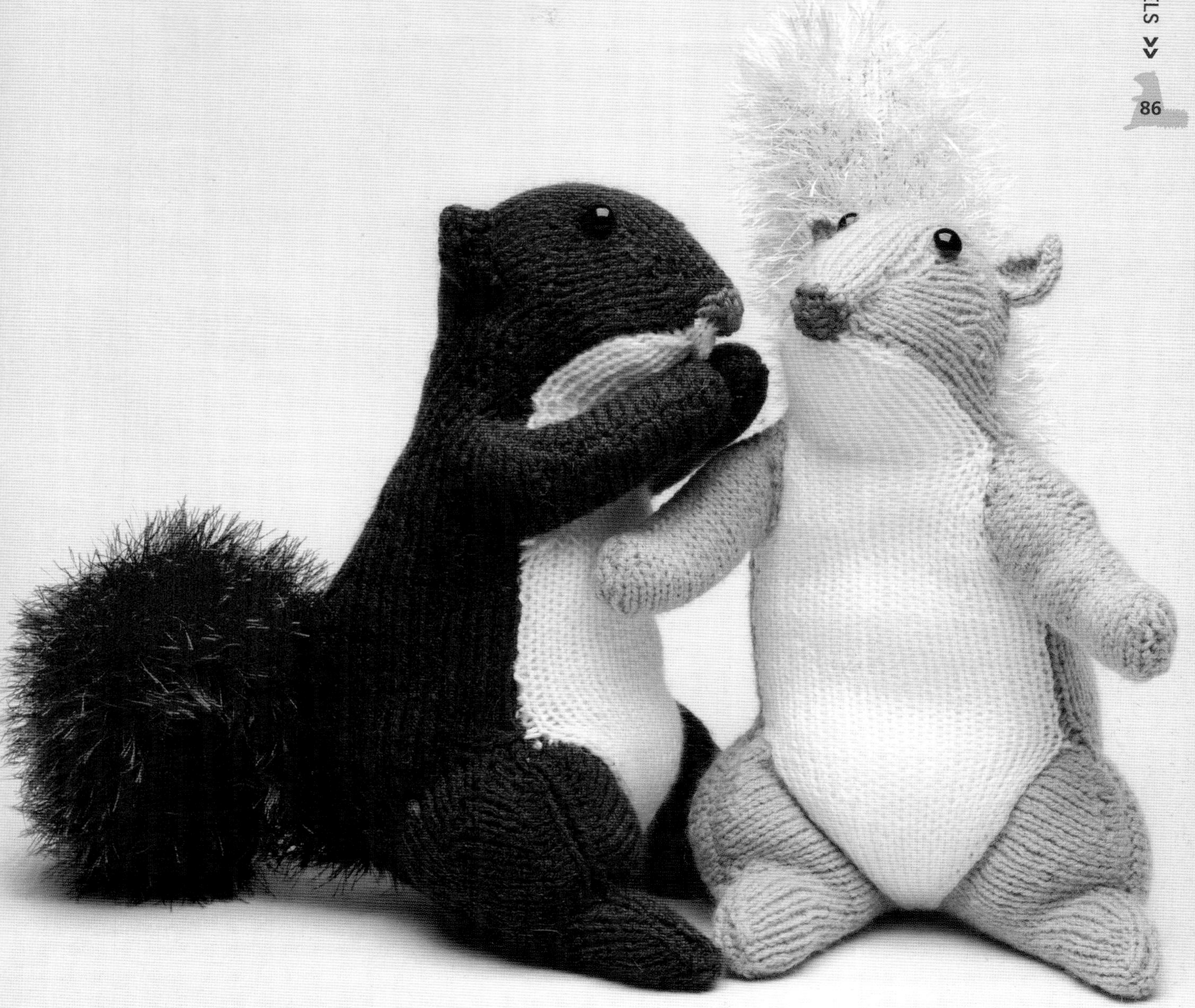

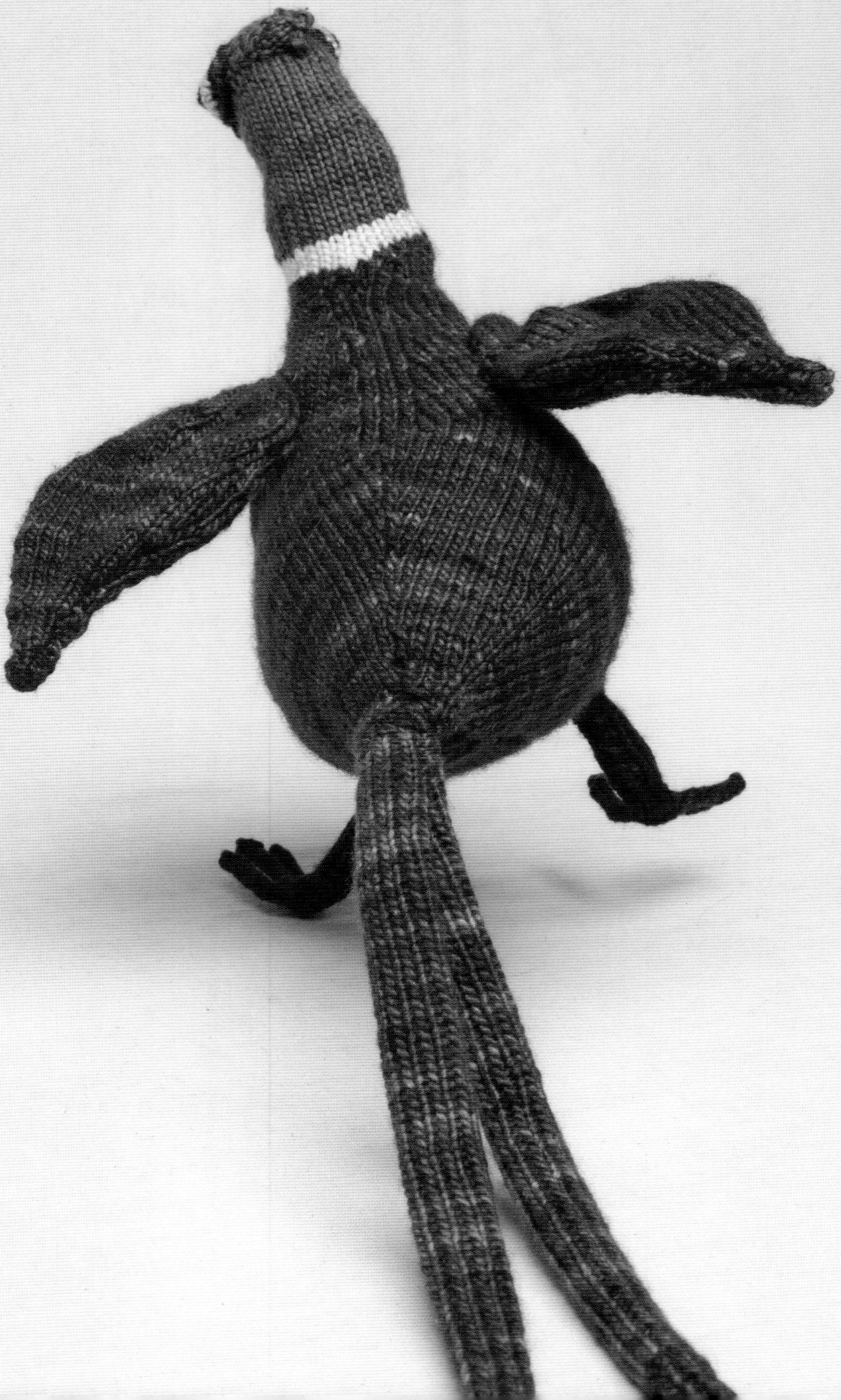

OWL >> 102

BEAR >> 106

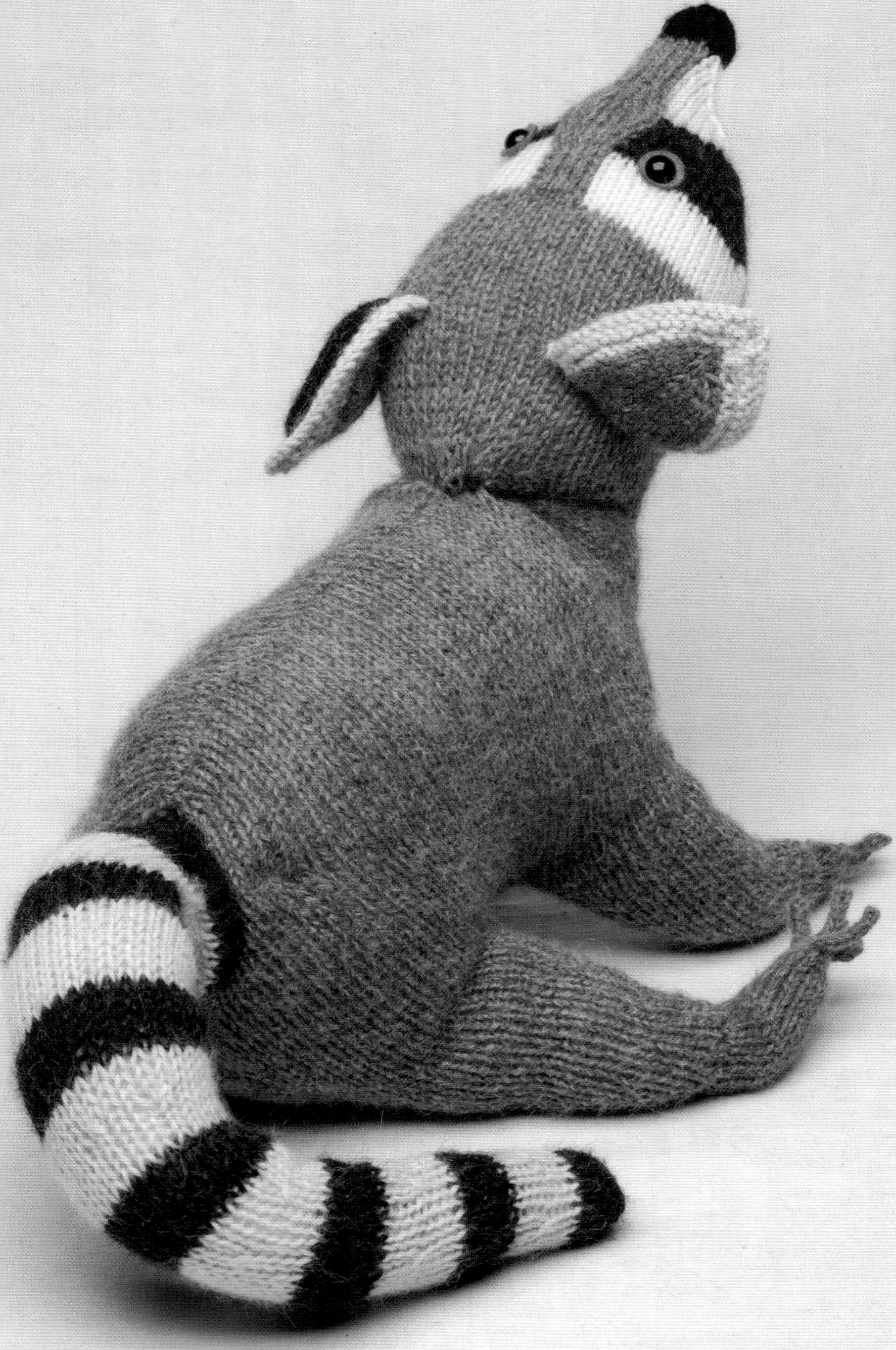

MISCHIEVOUS MOLE

Frolicsome frog

Pleasant pheasant

Ravenous rabbit

# The creatures

Beavers have large, sharp front teeth, clawed front feet, webbed back feet and large, flat, scaly tails. They are talented engineers, building elaborate homes called lodges in the banks of rivers and lakes, using logs and mud.

# BEAVER

**Did you know?**
Beavers move clumsily
on land but are extremely
graceful in the water.

# Information you'll need

### Finished size
Beaver measures approximately 14in
(36cm) from nose to tip of tail and body
is approximately 5½in (14cm) wide.

### Materials
Sublime Baby Cashmere Merino Silk DK,
75% extra fine merino, 20% silk, 5%
cashmere (127yds/116m per 50g ball):
1 x 50g ball in shade 0219 Carrots (A)
1 x 50g ball in shade 0218 Marmite (B)
Small amounts of DK yarn in beige (C),
black (D) and white (E)

Set of four 3.25mm (UK10:US3)
double-pointed needles
1 pair of 3.25mm (UK10:US3) needles
Polyester toy filling
Tapestry needle
2 x ⁵⁄₁₆in (8mm) black safety eyes

### Tension
24 sts and 32 rows to 4in (10cm),
measured over st st, using 3.25mm
needles. Use larger or smaller needles
if necessary to obtain correct tension.

# How to make Beaver

## Body (in one piece)

Using four 3.25mm double-pointed needles and A, cast on 6 sts and divide between three needles, using fourth needle to knit with.

**Round 1:** (Inc1, k1) 3 times (9 sts).
**Round 2:** Knit.
**Round 3:** (Inc1, k2) 3 times (12 sts).
**Round 4:** Knit.
**Round 5:** (Inc1, k1) 6 times (18 sts).
**Round 6:** (K2, inc1) 6 times (24 sts).
**Round 7:** (K3, inc1) 6 times (30 sts).
**Round 8:** (K4, inc1) 6 times (36 sts).
**Round 9:** Knit.
**Round 10:** (Inc1, k5) twice, (k5, inc1) twice, k12 (40 sts).
**Round 11:** (Inc1, k6) twice, (k6, inc1) twice, k12 (44 sts).
**Round 12:** (Inc1, k7) twice, (k7, inc1) twice, k12 (48 sts).
**Round 13:** (Inc1, k5) 3 times, (k5, inc1) 3 times, k12 (54 sts).
**Round 14:** Knit.
**Round 15:** (Inc1, k6) 3 times, (k6, inc1) 3 times, k12 (60 sts).
**Round 16:** Knit.
**Round 17:** (Inc1, k7) 3 times, (k7, inc1) 3 times, k12 (66 sts).

Begin working in short rows, as follows:

**Row 1:** K53, turn.
**Row 2:** P52, turn.
**Row 3:** K51, turn.
**Row 4:** P50, turn.
**Row 5:** K49, turn.
**Row 6:** P48, turn.
**Row 7:** K47, turn.
**Row 8:** P46, turn.
**Row 9:** K45, turn.
**Row 10:** P44, turn.
**Row 11:** K43, turn.
**Row 12:** P42, turn.
**Row 13:** K41, turn.
**Row 14:** P40, turn.
**Row 15:** K39, turn.
**Row 16:** P38, turn.
**Row 17:** K37, turn.
**Row 18:** P36, turn.
**Row 19:** K57; do not turn but resume working in rounds.

Knit 18 rounds.

**Round 19:** (Sl1, k1, psso, k7) 3 times, (k7, k2tog) 3 times, k12 (60 sts).
**Rounds 20 and 21:** Knit.
**Round 22:** (Sl1, k1, psso, k6) 3 times, (k6, k2tog) 3 times, k12 (54 sts).
**Rounds 23 and 24:** Knit.
**Round 25:** (Sl1, k1, psso, k5) 3 times, (k5, k2tog) 3 times, k12 (48 sts).
**Rounds 26 and 27:** Knit.
**Round 28:** (Sl1, k1, psso, k4) 3 times, (k4, k2tog) 3times, k12 (42 sts).
**Rounds 29–32:** Knit; do not turn work but begin working in short rows once more.

**Row 1:** K8, turn.
**Row 2:** P28, turn.
**Row 3:** K27, turn.
**Row 4:** P26, turn.
**Row 5:** K25, turn.
**Row 6:** P24, turn.
**Row 7:** K23, turn.
**Row 8:** P22, turn.
**Row 9:** K18; do not turn but resume working in rounds.

**Round 1:** K35, M1, (k1, M1) twice, k5 (45 sts).
**Round 2:** Knit.
**Round 3:** (K4, inc1) 9 times (54 sts).
**Rounds 4–6:** Knit.
**Round 7:** (K7, sl1, k1, psso) twice, (k2tog, k7) twice, k2tog, k14, sl1, k1, psso (48 sts).
**Rounds 8–10:** Knit.
**Round 11:** (K6, sl1, k1, psso) twice, (k2tog, k6) twice, k2tog, k12, sl1, k1, psso (42 sts).
**Rounds 12–14:** Knit.
**Round 15:** (K5, sl1, k1, psso) twice, (k2tog, k5) twice, k2tog, k10, sl1, k1, psso (36 sts).
**Rounds 16 and 17:** Knit.
**Round 18:** (K4, sl1, k1, psso) twice, (k2tog, k4) twice, k2tog, k8, sl1, k1, psso (30 sts).
**Rounds 19 and 20:** Knit.
**Round 21:** (K3, sl1, k1, psso) twice, (k2tog, k3) twice, k2tog, k6, sl1, k1, psso (24 sts).
**Round 22:** Knit.
Cast off.

## Snout

Using four 3.25mm double-pointed needles and C, cast on 6 sts and divide between three needles.

**Round 1:** (K1, inc1) 3 times (9 sts).
**Round 2:** (K2, inc1) 3 times (12 sts).
**Round 3:** (K3, inc1) 3 times (15 sts).
**Round 4:** (K4, inc1) 3 times (18 sts).
**Round 5:** (K5, inc1) 3 times (21 sts).
**Round 6:** (K6, inc1) 3 times (24 sts).
**Round 7:** Knit.
Cast off.

## Ears (make 2)

Using 3.25mm needles and A, cast on 3 sts.

**Row 1:** Knit.
**Row 2:** K1, inc1, k1 (4 sts).
**Row 3:** Knit.
**Row 4:** K1, (inc1) twice, k1 (6 sts).
**Row 5:** Knit.
**Row 6:** K2, (inc1) twice, k2 (8 sts).
**Row 7:** Knit.
**Row 8:** K6, turn.
**Row 9:** K4, turn.
**Row 10:** K3, turn.
**Row 11:** K2, turn.
**Row 12:** K1, turn.

*beaver*

**Q:** How do beavers connect with the internet?
**A:** They log on.

**Row 13:** Knit to end.
**Row 14:** K1, sl1, k1, psso, k2, k2tog, k1 (6 sts).
**Row 15:** (K2tog) 3 times.
Cast off.

## Front legs (make 2)

Using 3.25mm needles and A, cast on 8 sts.
Beg with a k row, work 9 rows in st st.
**Rows 10 and 11:** Knit.
Beg with a p row, work a further 7 rows in st st.
**Row 19:** (K1, inc1) 4 times (12 sts).
**Row 20:** Purl.
**Row 21:** (K2, inc1) 4 times (16 sts).
**Row 22:** Purl.
**Row 23:** (K3, inc1) 4 times (20 sts).
**Row 24:** Purl.
**Row 25:** (K4, inc1) 4 times (24 sts).
**Row 26:** Purl.
**Row 27:** (K3, inc1) 6 times (30 sts).
**Row 28:** Purl.
Cast off.

## Back legs (make 2)

Using 3.25mm needles and A, cast on 10 sts.
Beg with a k row, work 9 rows in st st.
**Rows 10 and 11:** Knit.
Beg with a p row, work a further 7 rows in st st.
**Row 19:** K1, inc1, k6, inc1, k1 (12 sts).
**Row 20:** Purl.
**Row 21:** (K2, inc1) 4 times (16 sts).
**Row 22:** Purl.
**Row 23:** (K3, inc1) 4 times (20 sts).
**Row 24:** Purl.
**Row 25:** (K4, inc1) 4 times (24 sts).
**Row 26:** Purl.
**Row 27:** (K3, inc1) 6 times (30 sts).
**Row 28:** Purl.

**Row 29:** (K4, inc1) 6 times (36 sts).
**Row 30:** Purl.
**Row 31:** K32, turn.
**Row 32:** P28, turn.
**Row 33:** K26, turn.
**Row 34:** P24, turn.
**Row 35:** K22, turn.
**Row 36:** P20, turn.
**Row 37:** K18, turn.
**Row 38:** P16, turn.
**Row 39:** K14, turn.
**Row 40:** P12, turn.
**Row 41:** Knit to end.
**Row 42:** Purl.
Cast off.

## Tail (make 2)

Using 3.25mm needles and B, cast on 10 sts.
**Row 1:** Purl.
**Row 2:** (K2, p2) twice, k2.
**Row 3:** (P2, k2) twice, p2.
**Row 4:** As row 3.
**Row 5:** As row 2.
**Row 6:** K1, M1, k1, p2, k2, p2, k1, M1, k1 (12 sts).
**Row 7:** K1, (p2, k2) twice, p2, k1.
**Row 8:** As row 7.
**Row 9:** P1, (k2, p2) twice, k2, p1.
**Row 10:** As row 9.
**Row 11:** As row 7.
**Row 12:** K1, M1, (p2, k2) twice, p2, M1, k1 (14 sts).
**Row 13:** (P2, k2) 3 times, p2.
**Row 14:** K1, M1, p1, (k2, p2) twice, k2, p1, M1, k1 (16 sts).
**Row 15:** P1, (k2, p2) 3 times, k2, p1.
**Row 16:** As row 15.
**Row 17:** K1, (p2, k2) 3 times, p2, k1.
**Row 18:** As row 17.
Rep rows 15–18 twice, then row 16 once more.

**Row 28:** K1, sl1, k1, psso, (p2, k2) twice, p2, k2tog, k1 (14 sts).
**Row 29:** (P2, k2) 3 times, p2.
**Row 30:** As row 29.
**Row 31:** (K2, p2) 3 times, k2.
**Row 32:** K1, p2tog, p1, k2, p2, k2, p1, p2tog, k1 (12 sts).
**Row 33:** P1, (k2, p2) twice, k2, p1.
**Row 34:** As row 33.
**Row 35:** K1, (p2, k2) twice, p2, k1.
**Row 36:** P1, p2tog, k2, p2, k2, p2tog, p1 (10 sts).
**Row 37:** (K2, p2) twice, k2.
**Row 38:** K1, p2tog, p1, k2, p1, p2tog, k1 (8 sts).
**Row 39:** P1, k2, p2, k2, p1.
Cast off in pattern.

## Front claws (make 4)

Using 3.25mm needles and B, cast on 12 sts.
Cast off.

## Back feet (make 2)

Using 3.25mm needles and B, cast on 3 sts.
**Row 1:** Purl.
**Row 2:** K1, inc2, k1 (5 sts).
**Row 3:** Purl.
**Row 4:** (K1, inc1) twice, k1 (7 sts).
**Row 5:** Purl.
**Row 6:** K2, inc1, k1, inc1, k2 (9 sts).
**Row 7:** (P1, k1) 4 times, p1.
**Row 8:** (K1, p1) 4 times, k1.
**Row 9:** As row 7.
Cast off 1 st, (transfer st from right-hand to left-hand needle, cast on 1 st, cast off 3 sts) 4 times.

# Making up

## Body and head

Stuff the body and head firmly but take care not to overstuff. Attach the eyes about 12 rows from the cast-off edge and about 6 stitches either side of the line of decreases that runs down the centre of the head. Stitch the cast-off edges of the snout and head together neatly, to join the two together. For the ears, run a tail of yarn along the row ends on one side and pull up to gather slightly and create a cupped shape, then stitch one ear in place on each side of the head.

## Legs and claws

Fold each leg in half lengthways, right sides together, and stitch the seam in backstitch. Fold the bottom part to the inside, along the garter-stitch ridge. For the front claws, use the tails of B to neaten the claws; fold each claw in half and stitch a pair of claws together at the fold. Insert one into the open end of each front leg and use a tail of A to secure the folded edges of the claws just inside the opening and then to stitch the gap closed at the base of the leg. Stuff the front legs, position one on either side of the body, and stitch in place. Insert the cast-on edge of a back foot into the end of each back leg. Add stuffing to each back leg, then stitch the legs in place on either side of the body, towards the back end.

## Tail

Cut a piece of foam slightly smaller than one of the tail pieces. Place this between the two tail pieces, like a sandwich, with right sides of the tail (the neater sides) facing outwards. Oversew the two tail pieces together all round, trapping the foam inside. Stitch the cast-on edges of the tail to the back end of the Beaver.

## Face

Thread a tapestry needle with a length of D and embroider a satin-stitch nose and two lines radiating out from the base of the nose, to denote the edges of the mouth. Embroider teeth using long straight stitches running downwards from the base of the nose, using E. Stitch a single straight stitch with D, through the centre of the teeth, to emphasize them.

Frogs are amphibians that love to spend their time submerged in a muddy pond or basking on a lily pad. A frog's sticky tongue is attached at the front of its mouth and is used to catch and swallow food.

# FROG

**Did you know?**
A frog sheds its skin once a week and then eats it.

frog

## Information you'll need

### Finished size
Frog body is 5½in (14cm) long and 2½in (6cm) wide at the widest point.

### Materials
Patons Diploma Gold DK, 55% Wool, 25% Acrylic, 20% Nylon (130yd/120m per 50g):
1 x 50g ball in shade 6228 Dark Green (A)
Patons Fairytale Colour 4 Me DK, 100% wool (98yd/90m per 50g ball):
1 x 50g ball in shade 4952 Light Green (B)
1 pair of 3.25mm (UK10:US3) needles
Polyester toy filling
Tapestry needle
Small scrap of white wool felt
Six-stranded embroidery thread, black and white
Crewel needle

### Tension
24 sts and 32 rows to 4in (10cm), measured over st st using 3.25mm needles. Use larger or smaller needles if necessary to obtain correct tension.

### Did you know?
A frog can see upwards, forwards and sideways at the same time.

# How to make Frog

## Upper body

Using 3.25mm needles and A, cast on 12 sts.

**Row 1:** Purl.
**Row 2 (RS):** (K4, M1) twice, k4 (14 sts).
**Row 3:** Purl.
**Row 4:** K4, M1, k6, M1, k4 (16 sts).
**Row 5:** Purl.
**Row 6:** K4, M1, k8, M1, k4 (18 sts).
**Row 7:** Purl.
**Row 8:** K14, turn.
**Row 9:** P10, turn.
**Row 10:** K9, turn.
**Row 11:** P8, turn.
**Row 12:** K7, turn.
**Row 13:** P6, turn.
**Row 14:** K5, turn.
**Row 15:** P4, turn.
**Row 16:** K to end.
**Row 17:** Purl all sts.
**Row 18:** Cast off but do not cut yarn or fasten off last st; with RS facing, pick up and knit 5 sts up side edge, 12 sts along cast-on edge and 6 sts down other side (24 sts).
**Row 19:** Purl.
**Row 20:** K1, sl1, k1, psso, k to last 3 sts, k2tog, k1 (22 sts).
Beg with a purl row, work 7 rows in st st.
**Row 28:** K1, inc1, k5, sl1, k1, psso, k4, k2tog, k5, inc1, k1.
**Row 29:** Purl.
Rep rows 28 and 29 twice.
**Row 34:** K1, sl1, k1, psso, k to last 3 sts, k2tog, k1 (20 sts).
Beg with a purl row, work 13 rows in st st.
**Row 48:** K1, sl1, k1, psso, k to last 3 sts, k2tog, k1.
**Row 49:** Purl.
Rep rows 48 and 49 once (16 sts).
**Row 52:** K3, sl1, k1, psso, k1, sl1, k1, psso, k2tog, k1, k2tog, k3 (12 sts).
**Row 53:** Purl.

**Row 54:** K2, (sl1, k1, psso) twice, (k2tog) twice, k2 (8 sts).
Cast off purlwise.

## Belly/underside

Using 3.25mm needles and B, cast on 6 sts.
**Row 1 (and every odd-numbered row):** Purl.
**Row 2 (RS):** K1, inc1, k2, inc1, k1 (8 sts).
**Row 4:** K1, inc1, k4, inc1, k1 (10 sts).
**Row 6:** K1, inc1, k6, inc1, k1 (12 sts).
**Row 8:** K1, inc1, k8, inc1, k1 (14) sts.
Beg with a purl row, work 5 rows in st st.
**Row 14:** K1, inc1, k10, inc1, k1 (16 sts).
**Row 16:** K1, inc1, k12, inc1, k1 (18 sts).
**Row 18:** K1, inc1, k14, inc1, k1 (20 sts).
Beg with a purl row, work 19 rows in st st.
**Row 38:** K1, sl1, k1, psso, k to last 3 sts, k2tog, k1.
**Row 39:** Purl.
Rep rows 38 and 39 once (16 sts).
**Row 42:** K3, sl1, k1, psso, k1, sl1, k1, psso, k2tog, k1, k2tog, k3 (12 sts).
**Row 43:** Purl.
**Row 44:** K2, (sl1, k1, psso) twice, (k2tog) twice, k3 (8 sts).
Cast off purlwise.

## Front legs (make 2)

Using 3.25mm needles and A, cast on 8 sts.
Beg with a purl row, work 5 rows in st st.
**Row 6:** K3, M1, k2, M1, k3 (10 sts).
Beg with a purl row, work 3 rows in st st.
**Row 10:** K9, turn.
**Row 11:** P8, turn.
**Row 12:** K7, turn.
**Row 13:** P6, turn.
**Row 14:** K5, turn.
**Row 15:** P4, turn.
**Row 16:** K3, turn.
**Row 17:** P2, turn.
**Row 18:** Knit to end.

Beg with a purl row, work 5 rows in st st.
**Row 24:** K3, M1, k4, M1, k3 (12 sts).
**Row 25:** Purl.
**Row 26:** Knit.
**Row 27:** Purl.
**Row 28:** K3, M1, k6, M1, k3 (14 sts).
**Row 29:** Purl.
Cast off.

## Back legs (make 2)

Follow instructions for front legs to the end of row 18.
Beg with a purl row, work 3 rows in st st.
**Row 22:** K3, M1, k4, M1, k3 (12 sts).
Beg with a purl row, work 3 rows in st st.
**Row 26:** K3, M1, k6, M1, k3 (14 sts).
**Row 27:** Purl.
**Row 28:** (K3, M1) twice, k2, (M1, k3) twice (18 sts).
Beg with a purl row, work 3 rows in st st.
Cast off.

## Front feet (make 2)

Using 3.25mm needles and B, cast on 7 sts.
Beg with a purl row, work 5 rows in st st.
**Row 6:** Cast off 2 sts, (transfer st from right-hand to left-hand needle, cast on 5 sts, cast off 6 sts, knitting each st tbl) 3 times, cast off rem 2 sts.

## Back feet (make 2)

Using 3.25mm needles and B, cast on 7 sts.
Beg with a purl row, work 11 rows in st st.
**Row 12:** Cast off 2 sts, (transfer st from right-hand to left-hand needle, cast on 5 sts, cast off 6 sts, knitting each st tbl) 3 times, cast off rem 2 sts.

### Eyes (make 2)

Using 3.25mm needles and A, cast on
4 sts.
**Row 1:** Purl.
**Row 2:** Inc1, k2, inc1 (6 sts).
**Row 3:** Purl.
**Row 4:** Inc1, k4, inc1 (8 sts).
Beg with a purl row, work 3 rows in st st.
**Row 8:** K2tog, k4, k2tog (6 sts).
**Row 9:** Purl.
**Row 10:** K2tog, k2, k2tog (4 sts).
**Row 11:** Purl.
Cast off.

## Making up
### Body and belly

With wrong sides of upper body and belly
together, oversew cast-on ends together,
then oversew cast-off edges together.
Turn inside out and stitch side seams in
backstitch, leaving a small opening in one
side for turning. Turn right sides out, stuff
firmly (but do not overstuff) and close the
opening using mattress stitch.

### Head

To shape the head, sew a running stitch
across the back of the neck, using B,
starting and finishing at the side seam,
then pull up to gather and shape the back
of the neck. Decide on the position of
the two eyes, then join the thread to the
position of one of the eye sockets and take
it through the head to the position of the
other eye socket, then stitch through the
same place several times more, pulling the
yarn just enough to create an indentation
on each side. (You can do this at the front
of the head, too, if you wish, to create a
dimpled shape, like two nostrils.)

### Eyes

To finish each eye, thread the tail of yarn
into the needle and sew a running stitch
around the perimeter of the piece, then
draw up the yarn to gather the shape into
a ball, adding some yarn ends or a little
stuffing to the inside as you do so.
Pull the yarn really tight and tuck in the
edges of the shape to create a neat,
small, tight ball. Fasten off and leave a
tail of yarn to sew each eyeball in place.
Cut two circles of white wool felt, ½in
(12mm) in diameter, place one on each
eye and oversew the edges using a crewel
needle and a single strand of white thread.
Thread the needle with two strands of
black thread and stitch a satin-stitch circle
in the centre of each white circle. Stitch
the eyes in place, positioning them in the
eye sockets you have created, and taking
the yarn right through the head so that the
eyes are secure.

### Legs and feet

Stitch the leg seams on each of the four
legs: to do this, fold the leg in half, with
wrong side out, and stitch seam using
backstitch, then turn right side out. Stuff
each leg, then stitch the top part to the
body, using the picture of the finished frog
as a guide to positioning. Neaten each
foot by oversewing the long edges of each
'finger' together, to make them narrower
and firmer, then fold in the edges of the
main piece, towards the centre, and stitch
neatly in place. Insert the feet into the
open ends of the legs and use A to stitch
them in place.

Rabbits have long ears and powerful back legs, useful for running, thumping the ground to warn of danger, and sometimes kicking. They spend most of the day hiding in vegetation or their underground burrows and feed mainly at night.

# RABBIT

# Information you'll need

### Finished size
Rabbit measures approximately 14½in (37cm) from nose to tail.

### Materials
King Cole Baby Alpaca DK, 100% Alpaca (110yd/100m per 50g ball):
3 x 50g balls in shade 504 Koala (A)
1 x 50g ball in shade 501 Fawn (B)
King Cole Merino Blend DK, 100% Wool (123yd/112m per 50g ball):
1 x 50g ball in shade 46 Aran (C)
King Cole Moments DK, 100% Polyester (98yd/90m per 50g ball):
1 x 50g ball in shade 471 Cream (D)
Small amount of black yarn
1 pair of 3.25mm (UK10:US3) needles
Set of four 3.25mm (UK10:US3) double-pointed needles
Polyester toy filling
Tapestry needle
2 x ⁵⁄₁₆in (8mm) black safety eyes

### Tension
24 sts and 32 rows to 4in (10cm), measured over st st using 3.25mm needles. Use larger or smaller needles if necessary to obtain correct tension.

*rabbit*

## Did you know?
Rabbits have almost 360° vision – they can even see behind them.

# How to make Rabbit

## Belly

Using 3.25mm needles and C, cast on 4 sts.

**Row 1:** Purl.
**Row 2:** K1, (inc1) twice, k1 (6 sts).
**Row 3:** Purl.
**Row 4:** K1, inc1, knit to last 2 sts, inc1, k1.
Rep rows 3 and 4 six times (20 sts).
Beg with a purl row, work 15 rows in st st.
**Row 32:** Knit all sts; place stitch markers at each end of this row.
Beg with a purl row, work a further 23 rows in st st.
**Row 56:** Knit all sts; place stitch markers at each end of this row.
**Row 57:** Purl.
**Row 58:** K1, sl1, k1, psso, knit to last 3 sts, k2tog, k1.
**Row 59:** Purl.
**Row 60:** Knit.
**Row 61:** Purl.
Rep rows 58–61 three times, then rows 58–59 once; place rem 12 sts on a holder, ready to make the head.

## Back body

Using 3.25mm needles and A, cast on 48 sts.

**Row 1:** Purl.
**Row 2:** K26, turn.
**Row 3:** P4, turn.
**Row 4:** K5, turn.
**Row 5:** P6, turn.
**Row 6:** K7, turn.
**Row 7:** P8, turn.
**Row 8:** K9, turn.
**Row 9:** P10, turn.
**Row 10:** K11, turn.
**Row 11:** P12, turn.
**Row 12:** K13, turn.
**Row 13:** P14, turn.
**Row 14:** K15, turn.
**Row 15:** P16, turn.
**Row 16:** K17, turn.
**Row 17:** P18, turn.
**Row 18:** K19, turn.
**Row 19:** P20, turn.
**Row 20:** K21, turn.
**Row 21:** P22, turn.
**Row 22:** K23, turn.
**Row 23:** P24, turn.
**Row 24:** K25, turn.
**Row 25:** P26, turn.
**Row 26:** K27, turn.
**Row 27:** P28, turn.
**Row 28:** K29, turn.
**Row 29:** P30, turn.
**Row 30:** K31, turn.
**Row 31:** P32, turn.
**Row 32:** K33, turn.
**Row 33:** P34, turn.
**Row 34:** K35, turn.
**Row 35:** P36, turn.
**Row 36:** K37, turn.
**Row 37:** P38, turn.
**Row 38:** K39, turn.
**Row 39:** P40, turn.
**Row 40:** K41, turn.
**Row 41:** P42, turn.
**Row 42:** K43, turn.
**Row 43:** P44, turn.
**Row 44:** Knit to end.
Beg with a purl row, work 15 rows in st st.
**Row 60:** K18, sl1, k1, psso, k8, k2tog, k18 (46 sts).
**Row 61:** Purl.
**Row 62:** K17, sl1, k1, psso, k8, k2tog, k17 (44 sts).
**Row 63:** Purl.
**Row 64:** K1, sl1, k1, psso, k13, sl1, k1, psso, k8, k2tog, k13, k2tog, k1 (40 sts).
**Row 65:** P14, p2tog tbl, p8, p2tog, p14 (38 sts).
**Row 66:** K36, turn.
**Row 67:** P34, turn.
**Row 68:** K32, turn.
**Row 69:** P30, turn.
**Row 70:** K28, turn.
**Row 71:** P26, turn.
**Row 72:** Knit to end.
**Row 73:** P13, p2tog tbl, p8, p2tog, p13 (36 sts).
**Row 74:** Cast on 19 sts, knit to end (55 sts).
**Row 75:** Cast on 19 sts, purl to end (74 sts).
**Row 76:** K1, inc1, k29, sl1, k1, psso, k8, k2tog, k29, inc1, k1.
**Row 77:** Purl.
**Row 78:** K31, sl1, k1, psso, k8, k2tog, k31 (72 sts).
**Row 79:** Purl.
**Row 80:** K1, sl1, k1, psso, k27, sl1, k1, psso, k8, k2tog, k27, k2tog, k1 (68 sts).
**Row 81:** Purl.
**Row 82:** K28, sl1, k1, psso, k8, k2tog, k28 (66 sts).
**Row 83:** Purl.
**Row 84:** Cast off 24 sts, knit to end (42 sts).
**Row 85:** Cast off 24 sts, purl to end (18 sts).
**Row 86:** Knit.
**Row 87:** Purl.
Do not cut yarn.

## Head

Continuing from neck edge of back body, commence working in rounds.

**Round 1:** Using 3.25mm double-pointed needles, k18 (placing 9 sts on each of two needles), then knit 12 sts from the holder on the neck end of belly, placing these sts on third needle, and use the fourth needle to knit with; do not turn.
**Round 4:** (K4, inc1) 4 times, k7, inc1, k4, inc1, k3 (42 sts).
**Round 5:** Knit.
**Round 6:** (K5, inc1) twice, k4, (inc1, k5)

twice, (k4, inc1) twice, k4 (48 sts).
**Rounds 7 and 8:** Knit.
Commence working in short rows.
**Row 1:** K30, turn.
**Row 2:** P28, turn.
**Row 3:** K27, turn.
**Row 4:** P26, turn.
**Row 5:** K25, turn.
**Row 6:** P24, turn.
**Row 7:** K23, turn.
**Row 8:** P22, turn.
**Row 9:** K21, turn.
**Row 10:** P20, turn.
**Row 11:** K19, turn.
**Row 12:** P18, turn.
**Row 13:** K17, turn.
**Row 14:** P16, turn.
**Row 15:** K15, turn.
**Row 16:** P14, turn.
**Row 17:** K13, turn.
**Row 18:** P12, turn.
**Row 19:** K11, turn.
**Row 20:** P10, turn.
**Row 21:** K38; do not turn but resume working in rounds.
**Rounds 1–4:** Knit.
**Round 5:** K33, sl1, k1, psso, k10, k2tog, k1 (46 sts).
**Round 6:** K33, sl1, k1, psso, k8, k2tog, k1 (44 sts).
**Round 7:** K33, sl1, k1, psso, k6, k2tog, k1 (42 sts).
**Round 8:** K33, sl1, k1, psso, k4, k2tog, k1 (40 sts).
**Round 9:** Knit.
**Round 10:** K9, sl1, k1, psso, k10, k2tog, k17 (38 sts).
**Round 11:** Knit.
**Round 12:** K8, sl1, k1, psso, k10, k2tog, k16 (36 sts).
**Round 13:** Knit.
**Round 14:** K7, sl1, k1, psso, k10, k2tog, k15 (34 sts).

**Round 15:** Knit.
**Round 16:** K6, sl1, k1, psso, k10, k2tog, k14 (32 sts).
**Round 17:** Knit.
**Round 18:** K5, sl1, k1, psso, k10, k2tog, k13 (30 sts).
**Round 19:** Knit.
**Round 20:** K4, sl1, k1, psso, k10, k2tog, k12 (28 sts).
Knit 6 rounds.
**Round 27:** Sl1, k1, psso, k2, sl1, k1, psso, k8, k2tog, k2, k2tog, k8 (24 sts).
**Round 28:** K1, (sl1, k1, psso) twice, k6, (k2tog) twice, k2, sl1, k1, psso, k2, k2tog, k1 (18 sts).
**Row 29:** K1, (sl1, k1, psso) twice, k2, (k2tog) twice, k2, sl1, k1, psso, k2tog, k1 (12 sts).
**Row 30:** (sl1, k1, psso) twice, (k2tog) twice, k4.
Cut yarn and thread tail through rem 8 sts.

## Left back outer leg
Using 3.25mm needles and A, with RS of the back body facing and cast-on edge uppermost, working from right to left, pick up and knit the first 22 sts of the cast-on edge.
**Row 2:** Purl.
**Row 3:** K20, turn.
**Row 4:** P18, turn.
**Row 5:** K17, turn.
**Row 6:** P16, turn.
**Row 7:** K15, turn.
**Row 8:** P14, turn.
**Row 9:** K13, turn.
**Row 10:** P12, turn.
**Row 11:** K11, turn.
**Row 12:** P10, turn.
**Row 13:** Knit to end.
**Row 14:** P18, turn.
**Row 15:** Knit to end.
**Row 16:** P17, turn.

**Row 17:** Knit to end.
**Row 18:** P16, turn.
**Row 19:** Knit to end.
**Row 20:** P15, turn.
**Row 21:** Knit to end.
**Row 22:** P14, turn.
**Row 23:** Knit to end.
**Row 24:** P13, turn.
**Row 25:** Knit to end.
**Row 26:** Purl.
**Row 27:** Cast off 10 sts, knit to end (12 sts).
**Row 28:** P9, p2tog, p1 (11 sts).
Beg with a knit row, work 11 rows in st st.
**Row 40:** P8, p2tog, p1 (10 sts).
**Row 41:** Knit.
**Row 42:** P7, p2tog, p1 (9 sts).
**Row 43:** Knit.
**Row 44:** P6, p2tog, p1 (8 sts).
**Row 45:** K1, sl1, k1, psso, k5.
Cast off rem 7 sts purlwise.

## Right back outer leg
Using 3.25mm needles and A, with RS of the back body facing and cast-on edge uppermost, miss next 4 sts after left leg, then pick up and knit 22 sts.
Follow instructions for the left back outer leg to end of row 13.
**Row 14:** Purl.
**Row 15:** K18, turn.
**Row 16:** Purl to end.
**Row 17:** K17, turn.
**Row 18:** Purl to end.
**Row 19:** K16, turn.
**Row 20:** Purl to end.
**Row 21:** K15, turn.
**Row 22:** Purl to end.

**Row 23:** K14, turn.
**Row 24:** Purl to end.
**Row 25:** K13, turn.
**Row 26:** Purl to end.
**Row 27:** Knit.
**Row 28:** Cast off 10 sts, purl to end (12 sts).
**Row 29:** K9, k2tog, k1 (11 sts).
Beg with a purl row, work 11 rows in st st.
**Row 41:** K8, k2tog, k1 (10 sts).
**Row 42:** Purl.
**Row 43:** K7, k2tog, k1 (9 sts).
**Row 44:** P1, p2tog, p6 (8 sts).
**Row 45:** K5, k2tog, k1.
Cast off rem 7 sts purlwise.

## Right back inner leg

Using 3.25mm needles and A, cast on 22 sts.
**Row 1:** Purl.
**Row 2:** Knit.
**Row 3:** P18, turn.
**Row 4:** Knit to end.
**Row 5:** P17, turn.
**Row 6:** Knit to end.
**Row 7:** P16, turn.
**Row 8:** Knit to end.
**Row 9:** P15, turn.
**Row 10:** Knit to end.
**Row 11:** P14, turn.
**Row 12:** Knit to end.
**Row 13:** P13, turn.
**Row 14:** Knit to end.
**Row 15:** Purl.
**Row 16:** Cast off 10 sts, knit to end (12 sts).
**Row 17:** P9, p2tog, p1 (11 sts).
Beg with a knit row, work 11 rows in st st.
**Row 29:** P8, p2tog, p1 (10 sts).
**Row 30:** Knit.
**Row 31:** P7, p2tog, p1 (9 sts).
**Row 32:** Knit.
**Row 33:** P6, p2tog, p1 (8 sts).

**Row 34:** K1, sl1, k1, psso, k5.
Cast off rem 7 sts purlwise.

## Left back inner leg

Using 3.25mm needles and A, cast on 22 sts.
**Row 1:** Purl.
**Row 2:** Knit.
**Row 3:** Purl.
**Row 4:** K18, turn.
**Row 5:** Purl to end.
**Row 6:** K17, turn.
**Row 7:** Purl to end.
**Row 8:** K16, turn.
**Row 9:** Purl to end.
**Row 10:** K15, turn.
**Row 11:** Purl to end.
**Row 12:** K14, turn.
**Row 13:** Purl to end.
**Row 14:** K13, turn.
**Row 15:** Purl to end.
**Row 16:** Knit.
**Row 17:** Cast off 10 sts, purl to end (12 sts).
**Row 18:** K9, k2tog, k1 (11 sts).
Beg with a purl row, work 11 rows in st st.
**Row 30:** K8, k2tog, k1 (10 sts).
**Row 31:** Purl.
**Row 32:** K7, k2tog, k1 (9 sts).
**Row 33:** P1, p2tog, p6 (8 sts).
**Row 34:** K5, k2tog, k1.
Cast off rem 7 sts purlwise.

## Left front paw

Using 3.25mm needles and A, cast on 19 sts.
**Row 1:** K17, inc1, k1 (20 sts).
**Row 2:** Purl.
**Row 3:** K1, inc1, k16, inc1, k1 (22 sts).
**Row 4:** Purl.
**Row 5:** K20, inc1, k1 (23 sts).
**Row 6:** Purl.
**Row 7:** K1, sl1, k1, psso, k18, inc1, k1.

**Row 8:** Purl.
**Row 9:** K21, inc1, k1 (24 sts).
**Row 10:** Purl.
Cast off.

## Right front paw

Using 3.25mm needles and A, cast on 19 sts.
**Row 1:** K1, inc1, knit to end (20 sts).
**Row 2:** Purl.
**Row 3:** K1, inc1, k16, inc1, k1 (22 sts).
**Row 4:** Purl.
**Row 5:** K1, inc1, knit to end (23 sts).
**Row 6:** Purl.
**Row 7:** K1, inc1, k18, k2tog, k1.
**Row 8:** Purl.
**Row 9:** K1, inc1, knit to end (24 sts).
**Row 10:** Purl.
Cast off.

## Ears (make 2)

Using 3.25mm needles and A, cast on 15 sts.
Beg with a purl row, work 31 rows in st st.
**Row 32:** K4, sl1, k1, psso, k3, k2tog, k4 (13 sts).
**Row 33 (and each odd-numbered row):** Purl.
**Row 34:** K3, sl1, k1, psso, k3, k2tog, k3 (11 sts).
**Row 36:** K2, sl1, k1, psso, k3, k2tog, k2 (9 sts).
**Row 38:** K1, sl1, k1, psso, k3, k2tog, k1 (7 sts).
**Row 40:** K1, sl1, k1, psso, k1, k2tog, k1.
Cast off rem 5 sts purlwise.

## Ear linings (make 2)

Using 3.25mm needles and B, cast on 13 sts.
Beg with a purl row, work 29 rows in st st.
**Row 30:** K3, sl1, k1, psso, k3, k2tog, k3 (11 sts).

**Row 31 (and each odd-numbered row):**
Purl.
**Row 32:** K2, sl1, k1, psso, k3, k2tog, k2
(9 sts).
**Row 34:** K1, sl1, k1, psso, k3, k2tog, k1
(7 sts).
**Row 36:** K1, sl1, k1, psso, k1, k2tog, k1
(5 sts).
**Row 38:** K1, sl1, k2tog, psso, k1.
Cast off rem 3 sts purlwise.

## Tail

Using 3.25mm needles and B, cast on
12 sts.
Beg with a purl row, work 15 rows in st st;
cut B and join in D.
Beg with a knit row, work 20 rows in st st.
Cast off.

## Making up

### Body

Stitch the tops of the inner legs and paws
to the belly between marked rows. Attach
the eyes to the head, using the picture
of the finished rabbit as a guide. (To help
with placement, stuff the head and mark
position of the eyes with pins, then remove
stuffing and insert eyes.) Place right sides
of back and underside of rabbit together
and stitch all round, leaving a gap between
the tops of the legs on one side. Turn right
sides out. Stuff the body and head firmly
but take care not to overstuff. Thread a
needle with a length of A and use this to
stitch through the head, from behind each
eye, to shape the head and make it slightly
narrower at this point.

### Tail and ears

Fold the tail in half, stitch the two sides of
the tail together, add a little stuffing, then
stitch the open edge to the back of the
body. Stitch the ear lining to each ear then
attach to the head, using the picture of the
finished rabbit as a guide to positioning.
Embroider the nose using black yarn.

Q: Why are rabbits like calculators?
A: They multiply really quickly.

Moles use their strong front paws for digging tunnels and scooping the earth backwards as they dig. They have black velvety fur, long, pointed noses, and sensitive whiskers to help guide them in the dark.

# MOLE

# Information you'll need

## Finished size
Mole measures approximately 11in (28cm) high from the tip of the tail to the end of the nose.

## Materials
Artesano Superwash Merino DK, 100% Merino Wool (122yd/112m per 50g):
1 x 50g ball in shade SFN50 Black (A)
Artesano DK 100% Alpaca, (109yd/100m per 50g)
1 x 50g ball in shade CA13 Sweet Pea (B)
Set of four 3.25mm (UK10:US3) double-pointed needles
Polyester toy filling
Tapestry needle
2 x ⁵⁄₁₆in (8mm) black safety eyes
Colourless nylon thread or fishing line

## Tension
24 sts and 32 rows to 4in (10cm), measured over st st using 3.25mm needles. Use larger or smaller needles if necessary to obtain correct tension.

# How to make Mole

## Tail, body and head (in one piece)

Using two 3.25mm double-pointed needles and A, cast on 2 sts.

**Row 1:** K2; do not turn but slide sts to other end of needle.

Rep row 1 six times.

**Row 8:** (Inc1) twice (4 sts).

**Row 9:** K4; do not turn but slide sts to other end of needle.

Rep row 9 three times.

**Row 13:** K1, (inc1) twice, k1 (6 sts). Divide the stitches between three double-pointed needles and, using the fourth needle to knit with, commence working in rounds.

**Rounds 1–8:** Knit.

**Round 9:** (K1, inc1) 3 times (9 sts).

**Round 10:** (K2, inc1) 3 times (12 sts).

**Round 11:** (K3, inc1) 3 times (15 sts).

**Round 12:** (K4, inc1) 3 times (18 sts).

**Round 13:** (K5, inc1) 3 times (21 sts).

**Round 14:** (K6, inc1) 3 times (24 sts).

**Round 15:** (K3, inc1) 6 times (30 sts).

**Round 16:** Knit.

**Round 17:** (K4, inc1) 6 times (36 sts).

**Round 18:** Knit.

**Round 19:** K12, (k4, inc1) 4 times, k4 (40 sts).

**Round 20:** Knit.

**Round 21:** K12, (k5, inc1) twice, k4, (1nc1, k5) twice (44 sts).

**Round 22:** Knit.

**Round 23:** K12, (k6, inc1) twice, k4, (inc1, k6) twice (48 sts).

Knit 23 rounds.

**Round 47:** K12, (k6, sl1, k1, psso) twice, k4, (k2tog, k6) twice (44 sts).

**Round 48:** Knit.

**Round 49:** K12, (k5, sl1, k1, psso) twice, k4, (k2tog, k5) twice (40 sts).

**Round 50:** Knit.

**Round 51:** K12, (k4, sl1, k1, psso) twice, k4, (k2tog, k4) twice (36 sts).

**Round 52:** Knit.

**Round 53:** (k4, k2tog) 6 times (30 sts).

**Round 54:** Knit.

**Round 55:** (k3, k2tog) 6 times (24 sts).

**Round 56:** K8, (k3, inc1) twice, (inc1, k3) twice (28 sts).

**Round 57:** K8, (k3, inc1) twice, k4, (inc1, k3) twice (32 sts).

**Round 58:** K8, (k4, inc1) twice, k4, (inc1, k4) twice (36 sts).

**Round 59:** K8, (k5, inc1) twice, k4, (inc1, k5) twice (40 sts).

Knit 7 rounds.

**Round 67:** K8, (k5, sl1, k1, psso) twice, k4, (k2tog, k5) twice (36 sts).

**Rounds 68 and 69:** Knit.

**Round 70:** K8, (k4, sl1, k1, psso) twice, k4, (k2tog, k4) twice (32 sts).

**Rounds 71 and 72:** Knit.

**Round 73:** K8, (k3, sl1, k1, psso) twice, k4, (k2tog, k3) twice (28 sts).

**Rounds 74 and 75:** Knit.

**Round 76:** K8, (k2, sl1, k1, psso) twice, k4, (k2tog, k2) twice (24 sts).

**Rounds 77 and 78:** Knit.

**Round 79:** (k2, k2tog) 6 times (18 sts).

**Round 80:** Knit.

Cast off.

## Snout

Using set of four 3.25mm double-pointed needles and B, cast on 6 sts; divide the stitches between three double-pointed needles and, using the fourth needle to knit with, commence working in rounds.

**Rounds 1–3:** Knit.

**Round 4:** (K1, inc1) 3 times (9 sts).

**Rounds 5 and 6:** Knit.

**Round 7:** (K2, inc1) 3 times (12 sts).

**Rounds 8 and 9:** Knit.

**Round 10:** (K1, inc1) 6 times (18 sts).

Knit 4 rounds.

Cast off.

## Front claws (make 2)

*Using two 3.25mm double-pointed needles and B, cast on 2 sts.

**Row 1:** K2; do not turn but slide sts to other end of needle.

Rep row 1 five times, cut yarn, leaving a tail, and transfer sts to a spare needle.** Rep from * to ** three times but do not cut yarn after fourth claw.

**Next row:** Knit across all stitches (8 sts).

**Next row:** Purl.

**Next row:** Cast on 2 sts, k to end (10 sts).

**Next row:** Cast on 2 sts, p to end (12 sts).
**Next row:** (Inc1) twice, k to last 2 sts, (inc1) twice (16 sts).
**Next row:** Inc1, p14, inc1 (18 sts).
Divide the stitches between three double-pointed needles and, using the fourth needle to knit with, commence working in rounds.
**Rounds 1–4:** Knit; cut B and join in A.
**Rounds 5 and 6:** Knit.
**Round 7:** (K5, inc1) 3 times (21 sts).
Knit 6 rounds.
**Round 14:** (K6, inc1) 3 times (24 sts).
Knit 3 rounds. Cast off.

## Back claws (make 4)
Using two 3.25mm double-pointed needles and B, cast on 2 sts.
**Row 1:** K2; do not turn but slide sts to other end of needle.
Rep row 1 eleven times. Cast off.

## Back legs (make 2)
Using set of four 3.25mm double-pointed needles and A, cast on 6 sts; divide the stitches between three double-pointed needles and, using the fourth needle to knit with, commence working in rounds.
**Round 1:** Knit.
**Round 2:** (K1, inc1) 3 times (9 sts).
Knit 9 rounds.
**Round 12:** Inc1, k7, inc1 (11 sts).
**Round 13:** Knit.
**Round 14:** Inc1, k9, inc1 (13 sts).
**Round 15:** Knit.
**Round 16:** Inc1, k11, inc1 (15 sts).
**Round 17:** Knit.
**Round 18:** Inc1, k13, inc1 (17 sts).
**Round 19:** Knit.
**Round 20:** Inc1, k15, inc1 (19 sts).
**Rounds 21 and 22:** Knit.
**Round 23:** Sl1, k1, psso, k15, k2tog (17 sts).

**Round 24:** Knit.
**Round 25:** Sl1, k1, psso, k13, k2tog (15 sts).
**Round 26:** Knit.
**Round 27:** Sl1, k1, psso, k11, k2tog (13 sts).
**Round 28:** Knit.
Cast off.

## Making up
### Body and head
Stuff the body and head firmly but take care not to overstuff. Attach eyes about 9 rows from the cast-off edge. On cast-on edge of snout, thread the tail of yarn into a tapestry needle and pass it through the end of the snout and pull through so that the first 2 rounds are tucked in. Stuff the snout, insert the cast-off edge into the front end of the head and oversew neatly to join the two together.

### Legs
On the front legs, use the tails of B to neaten the claws and to stitch the gap closed at the base of the claws. Stuff the front legs, position one on either side of the body with the paws facing backwards, and stitch in place. Fold each back claw in half and stitch two of these together at the fold, then insert this folded edge into the end of the back leg. Add a small amount of stuffing to each back leg. Stitch the legs in place on either side of the body, towards the back end.

### Whiskers
Insert lengths of nylon thread to form whiskers, adding a small blob of glue to the end, to hold it in place. You can do this before or after stitching the snout in place, whichever you find easier. (Note: if you are making the mole for a small child, omit the whiskers.)

## Did you know?
A mole weighs about the same as a medium-sized apple.

Snail move along slowly, carrying their house on their back – a coiled shell that they can retreat into when threatened by predators. Their bodies produce thick slime to allow them to crawl along without getting hurt.

# SNAIL

# Information you'll need

### Finished size
Snail measures 7in (17.5cm) long
and about 1½in (3.5cm) wide at the
widest point, and the shell measures
approximately 4in (10cm) in diameter.

### Materials
Manos del Uruguay Silk Blend DK, 70%
Merino, 30% Silk (300yd/270m per
100g skein)
1 x 100g skein in shade 2458 Indian (A)
1 x 100g skein in shade 2246
Mediterranean (B)

1 x 100g skein in shade 4949 Candy
Floss (C)
1 pair of 3.25mm (UK10:US3) needles
Polyester toy filling
Tapestry needle

### Tension
24 sts and 32 rows to 4in (10cm),
measured over st st using 3.25mm needles.
Use larger or smaller needles if necessary
to obtain correct tension.

**Did you know?**
Snails love wet conditions.
When it rains, they head off
to look for food.

# How to make Snail

## Top of body

Using 3.25mm needles and A, cast on 3 sts using two-needle method.
**Row 1 (RS):** K each st tbl.
**Row 2:** Purl.
**Row 3:** K1, inc2, k1 (5 sts).
**Row 4:** Purl.
**Row 5:** Knit.
**Row 6:** Purl.
**Row 7:** (K1, inc1) twice, k1 (7 sts).
Beg with a purl row, work 3 rows in st st.
**Row 11:** K1, inc1, k3, inc1, k1 (9 sts).
Beg with a purl row, work 3 rows in st st.
**Row 15:** K1, inc1, k5, inc1, k1 (11 sts).
Beg with a purl row, work 5 rows in st st.
**Row 21:** K1, inc1, k7, inc1, k1 (13 sts).
Beg with a purl row, work 5 rows in st st.
**Row 27:** K1, inc1, k9, inc1, k1 (15 sts).
Beg with a purl row, work 5 rows in st st.
**Row 33:** K1, inc1, k11, inc1, k1 (17 sts).
Beg with a purl row, work 5 rows in st st.
**Row 39:** K8, turn.
**Row 40:** Purl to end.
**Row 41:** K7, turn.
**Row 42:** Purl to end.
**Row 43:** K6, turn.
**Row 44:** Purl to end.
**Row 45:** K5, turn.
**Row 46:** Purl to end.
**Row 47:** K4, turn.
**Row 48:** Purl to end.
**Row 49:** K3, turn.
**Row 50:** Purl to end.
**Row 51:** Knit all sts.
**Row 52:** P8, turn.
**Row 53:** Knit to end.
**Row 54:** P7, turn.
**Row 55:** Knit to end.
**Row 56:** P6, turn.
**Row 57:** Knit to end.
**Row 58:** P5, turn.
**Row 59:** Knit to end.
**Row 60:** P4, turn.

**Row 61:** Knit to end.
**Row 62:** P3, turn.
**Row 63:** Knit to end.
**Row 64:** Purl all sts.
Beg with a knit row, work 4 rows in st st.
**Row 69:** K5, sl1, k1, psso, k3, k2tog, k5 (15 sts).
Beg with a purl row, work 3 rows in st st.
**Row 73:** K5, sl1, k1, psso, k1, k2tog, k5 (13 sts).
Beg with a purl row, work 3 rows in st st.
**Row 77:** K11, turn.
**Row 78:** P9, turn.
**Row 79:** K7, turn.
**Row 80:** P5, turn.
**Row 81:** K3, turn.
**Row 82:** P1, turn.
**Row 83:** Knit to end.
**Row 84:** Purl.
**Row 85:** K1, sl1, k1, psso, k7, k2tog, k1 (11 sts).
**Row 86:** Purl.
**Row 87:** K1, sl1, k1, psso, k5, k2tog, k1 (9 sts).
**Row 88:** (P2tog) twice, k1, (p2tog) twice. Cast off rem 5 sts.

## Underside of body

Using 3.25mm needles and B, cast on 2 sts using two-needle method.
**Row 1 (WS):** K each st tbl.
**Row 2:** Purl.
**Row 3:** (Inc1) twice (4 sts).
Beg with a purl row, work 3 rows in st st.
**Row 7:** K1, (inc1) twice, k1 (6 sts).
Beg with a purl row, work 3 rows in st st.
**Row 11:** K1, inc1, k2, inc1, k1 (8 sts).
Beg with a purl row, work 31 rows in st st.
**Row 43:** K4, M1, k4 (9 sts).
Beg with a purl row, work 21 rows in st st.
**Row 65:** K1, sl1, k1, psso, k3, k2tog, k1 (7 sts).
**Row 66:** Purl.

**Row 67:** K1, sl1, k1, psso, k1, k2tog, k1. Cast off rem 5 sts purlwise.

## Shell

Using 3.25mm needles and C, cast on 30 sts using two-needle method.
**Row 1 (RS):** K each st tbl.
**Row 2:** Purl.
**Row 3:** Knit.
**Row 4:** Purl.
**Row 5:** (K4, k2tog) 5 times (25 sts).
Beg with a purl row, work 11 rows in st st.
**Row 17:** K23, turn.
**Row 18:** P21, turn.
**Row 19:** K19, turn.
**Row 20:** P17, turn.
**Row 21:** K15, turn.
**Row 22:** P13, turn.
**Row 23:** K11, turn.
**Row 24:** P9, turn.
**Row 25:** Knit to end.
**Row 26:** Purl.
**Row 27:** K1, sl1, k1, psso, k to last 3 sts, k2 tog, k1 (23 sts).
Beg with a purl row, work 3 rows in st st.
**Row 31:** K21, turn.
**Row 32:** P19, turn.
**Row 33:** K17, turn.
**Row 34:** P15, turn.
**Row 35:** K13, turn.
**Row 36:** P11, turn.
**Row 37:** K9, turn.
**Row 38:** P7, turn.
**Row 39:** Knit to end.
**Row 40:** Purl.
**Row 41:** K1, sl1, k1, psso, k to last 3 sts, k2 tog, k1 (21 sts).
Beg with a purl row, work 3 rows in st st.
**Row 45:** K19, turn.
**Row 46:** P17, turn.
**Row 47:** K15, turn.
**Row 48:** P13, turn.
**Row 49:** K11, turn.

**Row 50:** P9, turn.
**Row 51:** K7, turn.
**Row 52:** P5, turn.
**Row 53:** Knit to end.
**Row 54:** Purl.
**Row 55:** K1, sl1, k1, psso, k to last 3 sts, k2 tog, k1 (19 sts).
Beg with a purl row, work 3 rows in st st.
**Row 59:** K17, turn.
**Row 60:** P15, turn.
**Row 61:** K13, turn.
**Row 62:** P11, turn.
**Row 63:** K9, turn.
**Row 64:** P7, turn.
**Row 65:** K5, turn.
**Row 66:** P3, turn.
**Row 67:** Knit to end.
**Row 68:** Purl.
**Row 69:** K1, sl1, k1, psso, k to last 3 sts, k2 tog, k1 (17 sts).
Beg with a purl row, work 3 rows in st st.
**Row 73:** K15, turn.
**Row 74:** P13, turn.
**Row 75:** K11, turn.
**Row 76:** P9, turn.
**Row 77:** K7, turn.
**Row 78:** P5, turn.
**Row 79:** K3, turn.
**Row 80:** P1, turn.
**Row 81:** Knit to end.
**Row 82:** Purl.
**Row 83:** K1, sl1, k1, psso, k to last 3 sts, k2 tog, k1 (15 sts).
**Row 84:** Purl.
**Row 85:** K13, turn.
**Row 86:** P11, turn.
**Row 87:** K9, turn.
**Row 88:** P7, turn.
**Row 89:** K5, turn.
**Row 90:** P3, turn.
**Row 91:** Knit to end.
**Row 92:** Purl.
**Row 93:** K1, sl1, k1, psso, k to last 3 sts,

k2 tog, k1 (13 sts).
**Row 94:** Purl.
**Row 95:** K11, turn.
**Row 96:** P9, turn.
**Row 97:** K7, turn.
**Row 98:** P5, turn.
**Row 99:** K3, turn.
**Row 100:** P1, turn.
**Row 101:** Knit to end.
**Row 102:** Purl.
**Row 103:** K1, sl1, k1, psso, k to last 3 sts, k2 tog, k1 (11 sts).
**Row 104:** Purl.
**Row 105:** K9, turn.
**Row 106:** P7, turn.
**Row 107:** K5, turn.
**Row 108:** P3, turn.
**Row 109:** Knit to end.
**Row 110:** Purl.
**Row 111:** K1, sl1, k1, psso, k to last 3 sts, k2 tog, k1 (9 sts).
**Row 112:** Purl.
**Row 113:** K7, turn.
**Row 114:** P5, turn.
**Row 115:** K3, turn.
**Row 116:** P1, turn.
**Row 117:** Knit to end.
**Row 118:** Purl.
**Row 119:** K1, sl1, k1, psso, k3, k2 tog, k1 (7 sts).
**Row 120:** Purl.
**Row 121:** K5, turn.
**Row 122:** P3, turn.
**Row 123:** Knit to end.
**Row 124:** Purl.
**Row 125:** K1, sl1, k1, psso, k1, k2 tog, k1 (5 sts).
Beg with a purl row, work 3 rows in st st.
**Row 129:** Sl1, k1, psso, k1, k2tog (3 sts).
**Row 130:** Purl.
Cast off.

## Eye stalks (make 2)
Using 3.25mm needles and A, cast on 20 sts, using two-needle or cable method.
**Row 1:** K each st tbl.
Cast off.

# Making up
## Body
With purl side of upper body and knit side of the underside together, oversew the cast-on ends together, then oversew cast-off edges together. Stitch side seams in backstitch, using A and stitching one stitch in from the edges, to form a ridge all round; the grey yarn will be visible on the underside. Leave a small opening in one of the side seams, for stuffing. Stuff firmly (but do not overstuff) and stitch the opening closed.

## Shell
To make up the shell, fold in half lengthways, with right sides (knit side) together and stitch side seam in backstitch. Turn right sides out and stuff. Stitch cast-on edge, which forms base of shell, to top of body, then coil the shell and secure with a number of stitches, taking some of these right through the shell to make it really firm.

## Eyes
Fold each eye stalk in half lengthways and oversew long edges. Fold over about ⅛in (3mm) at one end of each, to form the eye, then stitch the base of each eye stalk to the head.

*snail*

Badgers live in an underground home called a sett, which comprises lots of interlocking tunnels. A family group of around six badgers lives together in a sett. Badgers like to come out at night to hunt for their favourite food: earthworms.

# BADGER

# Information you'll need

### Finished size
Badger measures approximately 21½in (55cm) from nose to tip of tail; body measures approximately 8in (20cm) wide.

### Materials
Debbie Bliss Rialto DK, 100% Merino (115yd/105m per 50g ball):
2 x 50g balls in shade 004 Grey (A)
2 x 50g balls in shade 003 Black (B)
1 x 50g ball in shade 002 Ecru (C)
Set of four 3.25mm (UK10:US3) double-pointed needles
1 pair of 3.25mm (UK10:US3) needles
Polyester toy filling
Tapestry needle
Small scrap of grey felt
2 x $\frac{7}{16}$in (11mm) blue safety eyes

### Tension
24 sts and 32 rows to 4in (10cm), measured over st st using 3.25mm needles. Use larger or smaller needles if necessary to obtain correct tension.

## Did you know?
Badgers are great housekeepers. They clean out their sleeping areas to get rid of lice and fleas.

# How to make Badger

## Upper body and head (in one piece)

Using 3.25mm needles and A, cast on 15 sts.

**Row 1 (and every odd-numbered row, unless stated):** Purl.

**Row 2:** K1, inc1, k5, M1, k1, M1, k5, inc1, k1 (19 sts).

**Row 4:** K1, inc1, k6, M1, k3, M1, k6, inc1, k1 (23 sts).

**Row 6:** K1, inc1, k7, M1, k5, M1, k7, inc1, k1 (27 sts).

**Row 8:** K1, inc1, k8, M1, k7, M1, k8, inc1, k1 (31 sts).

**Row 10:** K1, inc1, k9, M1, k9, M1, k9, inc1, k1 (35 sts).

**Row 12:** K1, inc1, k10, M1, k11, M1, k10, inc1, k1 (39 sts).

**Row 14:** K1, inc1, k11, M1, k13, M1, k11, inc1, k1 (43 sts).

**Row 16:** K1, inc1, k12, M1, k15, M1, k12, inc1, k1 (47 sts).

**Row 18:** K1, inc1, k13, M1, k17, M1, k13, inc1, k1 (51 sts).

**Row 20:** K1, inc1, k14, M1, k19, M1, k14, inc1, k1 (55 sts).

**Row 22:** K1, inc1, k15, M1, k21, M1, k15, inc1, k1 (59 sts).

**Row 24:** K1, inc1, k16, M1, k23, M1, k16, inc1, k1 (63 sts).

**Row 26:** K60, turn.
**Row 27:** P57, turn.
**Row 28:** K55, turn.
**Row 29:** P53, turn.
**Row 30:** K51, turn.
**Row 31:** P49, turn.
**Row 32:** K47, turn.
**Row 33:** P45, turn.
**Row 34:** K43, turn.
**Row 35:** P41, turn.
**Row 36:** K39, turn.
**Row 37:** P37, turn.
**Row 38:** K35, turn.
**Row 39:** P33, turn.
**Row 40:** K31, turn.
**Row 41:** P29, turn.
**Row 42:** K27, turn.
**Row 43:** P25, turn.
**Row 44:** K23, turn.
**Row 45:** P21, turn.
**Row 46:** K19, turn.
**Row 47:** P17, turn.
**Row 48:** K16, turn.
**Row 49:** P15, turn.
**Row 50:** Knit to end.

Beg with a p row, work 21 rows in st st.

**Row 72:** K24, sl1, k1, psso, k11, k2tog, k24 (61 sts).

**Row 73:** Purl.

**Row 74:** K23, sl1, k1, psso, k11, k2tog, k23 (59 sts).

Beg with a p row, work 7 rows in st st.

**Row 82:** K24, turn.
**Row 83:** Purl to end.
**Row 84:** k22, turn.
**Row 85:** Purl to end.
**Row 86:** K20, turn.
**Row 87:** Purl to end.
**Row 88:** K18, turn.
**Row 89:** Purl to end.
**Row 90:** Knit.
**Row 91:** P24, turn.
**Row 92:** Knit to end.
**Row 93:** P22, turn.
**Row 94:** Knit to end.
**Row 95:** P20, turn.
**Row 96:** Knit to end.
**Row 97:** P18, turn.
**Row 98:** Knit to end.
**Row 99:** Purl.

**Row 100:** K1, sl1, k1, psso, k19, sl1, k1, psso, k11, k2tog, k19, k2tog, k1 (55 sts).

Beg with a p row, work 3 rows in st st.

**Row 104:** K1, sl1, k1, psso, k17, sl1, k1, psso, k11, k2tog, k17, k2tog, k1 (51 sts).

Beg with a p row, work 3 rows in st st.

**Row 108:** K1, sl1, k1, psso, k15, sl1, k1, psso, k11, k2tog, k15, k2tog, k1 (47 sts).

**Row 109:** Purl.

**Row 110:** K1, sl1, k1, psso, k13, sl1, k1, psso, k11, k2tog, k13, k2tog, k1 (43 sts).

**Row 111:** Purl.

**Row 112:** K1, (sl1, k1, psso, k11) twice, k2tog, k11, k2tog, k1 (39 sts).

**Row 113:** Purl.

**Row 114:** K1, sl1, k1, psso, k9, sl1, k1, psso, k11, k2tog, k9, k2tog, k1 (35 sts).

**Row 115:** Purl.

**Row 116:** K1, sl1, k1, psso, k7, sl1, k1, psso, k11, k2tog, k7, k2tog, k1 (31 sts).

**Row 117:** Purl; cut A and join in C.

## Shape head

Beg with a k row, work 6 rows in st st.

**Row 7:** K10, M1, k11, M1, k10 (33 sts).

Beg with a p row, work 5 rows in st st.

**Row 13:** K31, turn.
**Row 14:** P29, turn.
**Row 15:** K27, turn.
**Row 16:** P25, turn.
**Row 17:** K23, turn.
**Row 18:** P21, turn.
**Row 19:** K19, turn.
**Row 20:** P17, turn.
**Row 21:** K15, turn.
**Row 22:** P13, turn.
**Row 23:** Knit to end.
**Row 24:** Purl.
**Row 25:** (K11, M1) twice, k11 (35 sts).
**Row 26:** Purl.
**Row 27:** K12, M1, k11, M1, k12 (37 sts).
**Row 28:** Purl.
**Row 29:** K13, M1, k11, M1, k13 (39 sts).
**Row 30:** Purl.
**Row 31:** K14, M1, k11, M1, k14 (41 sts).
**Row 32:** Purl.
**Row 33:** K1, inc1, k13, M1, k11, M1, k13, inc1, M1 (45 sts).

Beg with a p row, work 3 rows in st st.

**Row 37:** K1, sl1, k1, psso, k12, sl1, k1, psso, k11, k2tog, k12, k2tog, k1 (41 sts).
**Row 38:** Purl.
**Row 39:** K1, sl1, k1, psso, k11, sl1, k1, psso, k9, k2tog, k11, k2tog, k1 (37 sts).
**Row 40:** Purl.
**Row 41:** K1, (sl1, k1, psso, k9) twice, k2tog, k9, k2tog, k1 (33 sts).
**Row 42:** Purl.
**Row 43:** K1, sl1, k1, psso, k7 sl1, k1, psso, k9, k2tog, k7, k2tog, k1 (29 sts).
**Row 44:** Purl.
**Row 45:** K1, sl1, k1, psso, k5, sl1, k1, psso, k9, k2tog, k5, k2tog, k1 (25 sts).
**Row 46:** Purl.
**Row 47:** K1, sl1, k1, psso, k3, sl1, k1, psso, k9, k2tog, k3, k2tog, k1 (21 sts).
**Row 48:** Purl.
**Row 49:** (K1, sl1, k1, psso) 3 times, k3, (k2tog, k1) 3 times (15 sts).
Beg with a p row, work 3 rows in st st.
**Row 53:** K1, (sl1, k1, psso) 3 times, k1, (k2tog) 3 times, k1 (9 sts).
**Row 54:** Purl.
**Row 55:** Knit.
**Row 56:** (P3tog) 3 times.
Cut yarn and thread tail through rem 3 sts.

## Lower body and head

Using 3.25mm needles and B, cast on 15 sts.
**Row 1 (WS):** Purl.
**Row 2:** Knit.
**Row 3:** Purl.
**Row 4:** K1, inc1, k to last 2 sts, inc1, k1.
Rep rows 1–4 three times (23 sts).
Beg with a p row, work 65 rows in st st.
**Row 82:** K1, sl1, k1, psso, k to last 3 sts, k2tog, k1.
**Row 83:** Purl.
Rep rows 82 and 83 once more; place a marker on each end of this row.
Beg with a k row, work 24 rows in st st.

**Row 110:** K1, sl1, k1, psso, k to last 3 sts, k2tog, k1.
**Row 111:** Purl.
**Row 112:** Knit.
**Row 113:** Purl.
Rep rows 110–113 three times, then rows 110–112 once more.
**Row 129:** (P3tog) 3 times.
Cut yarn and thread tail through rem 3 sts.

## Tail

Using 3.25mm needles and A, cast on 15 sts.
**Row 1:** Purl.
**Row 2 (RS):** K1, sl1, k1, psso, k9, k2tog, k1 (13 sts).
Beg with a p row, work 3 rows in st st.
**Row 6:** K5, sl1, k2tog, psso, k5 (11 sts).
Beg with a p row, work 3 rows in st st.
**Row 10:** K4, sl1, k2tog, psso, k4 (9 sts).
**Row 11:** Purl.
**Row 12:** K1, sl1, k1, psso, sl1, k2tog, psso, k2tog, k1 (5 sts).
**Row 13:** Purl.
**Row 14:** K1, sl1, k2tog, psso, k1 (3 sts).
**Row 15:** P3tog; cut yarn and fasten off.

## Legs (make 4)

Using 3.25mm needles and B, cast on 30 sts.
**Row 1 (RS):** Knit.
**Row 2:** Purl.
**Row 3:** K28, turn.
**Row 4:** P26, turn.
**Row 5:** K24, turn.
**Row 6:** P22, turn.
**Row 7:** K20, turn.
**Row 8:** P18, turn.
**Row 9:** K16, turn.
**Row 10:** P14, turn.
**Row 11:** K12, turn.
**Row 12:** P10, turn.
**Row 13:** Knit to end.

Beg with a p row, work 7 rows in st st.
**Row 21:** (Sl1, k1, psso, k3) 3 times, (k3, k2tog) 3 times (24 sts).
Beg with a p row, work 3 rows in st st.
**Row 25:** (Sl1, k1, psso, k2) 3 times, (k2, k2tog) 3 times (18 sts).
Beg with a p row, work 3 rows in st st.
**Row 29:** K13, turn and leave rem 5 sts on a stitch holder.
**Row 30:** P8, turn and leave rem 5 sts on a stitch holder; place a marker in last st worked.
Work 8 rows on the centre 8 sts; cut yarn.
**Row 39:** Rejoin yarn to marked st from row 30; with RS facing, pick up and knit 5 sts evenly up right-hand edge, k8 sts from left-hand needle; pick up and knit 5 sts down opposite edge, then knit 5 sts from holder; turn (23 sts).
**Row 40:** P23, then purl 5 sts from holder (28 sts).
**Row 41:** Knit.
**Row 42:** Purl.
**Row 43:** K1, sl1, k1, psso, k4, (sl1, k1, psso, k1) twice, k2, (k1, k2tog) twice, k4, k2tog, k1 (22 sts).
**Row 44:** Purl; cut B; join in A.
**Row 45:** K1, sl1, k1, psso, k4, (sl1, k1, psso) twice, (k2tog) twice, k4, k2tog, k1 (16 sts).
**Row 46:** Purl.
**Row 47:** K4, (sl1, k1, psso) twice, (k2tog) twice, k4 (12 sts).
**Row 48:** Purl.
Cast off.

*badger*

## Head stripe (right)

Using 3.25mm needles and B, cast on 2 sts.
**Row 1 (and every odd-numbered row):** Purl.
**Row 2 (RS):** Knit.
**Row 4:** K1, M1, k1 (3 sts).
Beg with a p row, work 5 rows in st st.
**Row 10:** K1, M1, k2 (4 sts).
Beg with a p row, work 5 rows in st st.
**Row 16:** K1, M1, k3 (5 sts).
Beg with a p row, work 5 rows in st st.
**Row 22:** K1, M1, k4 (6 sts).
Beg with a p row, work 5 rows in st st.
**Row 28:** K1, M1, k5 (7 sts).
Beg with a p row, work 5 rows in st st.
**Row 34:** K1, M1, k6 (8 sts).
Beg with a p row, work 5 rows in st st.
**Row 40:** K1, M1, k7 (9 sts).
Beg with a p row, work 19 rows in st st.
Cast off.

## Head stripe (left)

Follow instructions for Head stripe (right) to the end of row 4.
Beg with a p row, work 5 rows in st st.
**Row 10:** K2, M1, k1 (4 sts).
Beg with a p row, work 5 rows in st st.
**Row 16:** K3, M1, k1 (5 sts).
Beg with a p row, work 5 rows in st st.
**Row 22:** K4, M1, k1 (6 sts).
Beg with a p row, work 5 rows in st st.
**Row 28:** K5, M1, k1 (7 sts).
Beg with a p row, work 5 rows in st st.
**Row 34:** K6, M1, k1 (8 sts).
Beg with a p row, work 5 rows in st st.
**Row 40:** K7, M1, k1 (9 sts).
Beg with a p row, work 19 rows in st st.
Cast off.

## Snout

Using set of four 3.25mm double-pointed needles and B, cast on 6 sts and divide between three needles, using fourth needle to knit with.

**Round 1:** (K1, inc1) 3 times (9 sts).
**Round 2:** (K2, inc1) 3 times (12 sts).
**Round 3:** (K3, inc1) 3 rimes (15 sts).
**Round 4:** (K4, inc1) 3 times (18 sts).
**Round 5:** (K2, inc1) 6 times (24 sts); cut B and join in C.
**Round 6:** Knit.
**Round 7:** (K3, inc1) 6 times (30 sts).
Knit 4 rounds.
**Round 12:** (K4, inc1) 6 times (36 sts).
Knit 6 rounds.
Cast off.

## Outer ears (make 2)

Using 3.25mm needles and C, cast on 7 sts.
**Row 1 (WS):** Purl.
**Row 2:** K1, inc1, k3, inc1, k1 (9 sts).
**Row 3:** Purl.
**Row 4:** K1, inc1, k5, inc1, k1 (11 sts).
Beg with a p row, work 3 rows in st st.
**Row 8:** K1, sl1, k1, psso, k5, k2tog, k1 (9 sts).
**Row 9:** Purl.
**Row 10:** K1, sl1, k1, psso, k3, k2tog, k1 (7 sts).
**Row 11:** Purl.
Cast off.

## Inner ears (make 2)

Using 3.25mm needles and B, cast on 6 sts.
**Row 1 (WS):** Purl.
**Row 2:** K1, inc1, k2, inc1, k1 (8 sts).
**Row 3:** Purl.
**Row 4:** K1, inc1, k4, inc1, k1 (10 sts).
Beg with a p row, work 3 rows in st st.
**Row 8:** K1, sl1, k1, psso, k4, k2tog, k1 (8 sts).
**Row 9:** Purl.
**Row 10:** K1, sl1, k1, psso, k2, k2tog, k1 (6 sts).
Cast off purlwise.

# Making up
## Body and head

Stitch top body and head to lower body and head, matching marked stitch on lower body to colour change between upper body and the head and leaving four gaps in the side seams for leg openings. Stuff head and partially stuff body. Pin the head stripes in place, starting at the neck where the colour change occurs; if stripes are too long, fold over excess to wrong side on opening at front of head. Stitch stripes to head.

## Eyes

Cut two circles of grey felt, slightly larger in diameter than the eyes; snip a small hole in the centre of each one. Push eye posts through the holes in the felt, then through both thicknesses of knitted fabric, about 12 rows up from the front edge, following the picture of the finished Badger as a guide to placement. Make sure the eyes are firmly secured. Stuff the snout and place the cast-off edge of the snout over the front end of the head and stitch neatly in place.

## Snout

For the ears, join in pairs, with right sides out and stitch inner ear to outer ear using tails of C and stuffing other yarn tails inside, to provide a little bit of padding.

## Legs and tail

Fold each leg in half lengthways, right sides out, and stitch the seam along the underneath of the foot in mattress stitch, then turn inside out and stitch leg seam in backstitch. Stuff two legs and stitch cast-off edges to leg openings towards front of body. Stuff two remaining legs and stitch cast-off edges to leg openings towards back end of body. Stitch tail in place.

Deer like to shelter in woodlands and graze on open land nearby. They are herbivores, feeding on grass, stems, berries and wild fruit. The spotted pattern on a deer's coat provides camouflage by helping it to blend in with the light and shadows in the forest.

# DEER

# Information you'll need

### Finished size
Deer measures approximately 18½in (47cm) from the nose to the tip of the tail.

### Materials
Debbie Bliss Baby Cashmerino, 55% Merino, 33% Microfibre, 12% Cashmere (135yd/125m per 50g ball):
2 x 50g balls in shade 63 Apricot (A)
1 x 50g ball each in 48 Fudge (B), and 100 White (C)
Small amount of black DK yarn
1 pair of 3.25mm (UK10:US3) needles
Stitch holders
Polyester toy filling
Tapestry needle
2 x ½in (12mm) brown safety eyes

### Tension
24 sts and 32 rows to 4in (10cm), measured over st st using 3.25mm needles. Use larger or smaller needles if necessary to obtain correct tension.

**Did you know?**
A fawn takes its first step just 20 minutes after being born.

deer

## How to make Deer

**Leg 1 (make 4)**
*Using 3.25mm needles and B, cast on 6 sts.
**Row 1 (WS):** Purl.
**Row 2:** K1, M1, k4, M1, k1 (8 sts).
**Row 3:** Purl.
**Row 4:** K1, M1, k6, M1, k1 (10 sts).
Beg with a purl row, work 3 rows in st st; cut B and join in A.
Beg with a knit row, work 26 rows in st st.**
**Row 34:** K1, M1, k to last st, M1, k1.
**Row 35:** Purl.

**Row 36:** K1, M1, knit to end.
**Row 37:** Purl.
Rep rows 34–37 twice more (19 sts).
Cut yarn and transfer to a stitch holder.

**Leg 2 (make 4)**
As Leg 1 from * to **.
**Row 34:** K1, M1, k to last st, M1, k1.
**Row 35:** Purl.
**Row 36:** K1, knit to last st, M1, k1.
**Row 37:** Purl.
Rep rows 34–37 twice more.
Cut yarn and transfer to a stitch holder.

**Left side**
Using 3.25mm needles and A, knit across the first 18 sts of a Leg 2, M1, k rem st, turn and cast on 8 sts, then knit the first st of Leg 1, M1, k to end (48 sts).
**Row 2:** Purl.
**Row 3:** K1, M1, knit to last st, M1, k1 (50 sts).
Beg with a purl row, work 3 rows in st st.
**Row 7:** K1, M1, knit to last st, M1, k1 (52 sts).
Beg with a purl row, work 3 rows in st st.
**Row 11:** Knit to last st, M1, k1 (53 sts).
Beg with a purl row, work 3 rows in st st.
**Row 15:** Knit to last st, M1, k1 (54 sts).
**Row 16:** Purl.
**Row 17:** K1, sl1, k1, psso, knit to last 3 sts, k2tog, k1.
**Row 18:** Purl.
**Row 19:** Knit to last 3 sts, k2tog, k1.
**Row 20:** Purl.
Rep rows 17–20 twice more.
Cast off rem 45 sts.

**Right side**
As Left side to end of row 10.
**Row 11:** K1, M1, knit to end (53 sts).
Beg with a purl row, work 3 rows in st st.
**Row 15:** K1, M1, knit to end (54 sts).
**Row 16:** Purl.
**Row 17:** K1, sl1, k1, psso, knit to last 3 sts, k2tog, k1.
**Row 18:** Purl.
**Row 19:** K1, sl1, k1, psso, knit to end.
**Row 20:** Purl.
Rep rows 17–20 twice more.
Cast off rem 45 sts.

## Belly

Using 3.25mm needles and C, cast on
2 sts.

**Row 1:** Purl.
**Row 2:** (Inc1) twice (4 sts).
**Row 3:** Purl.
**Row 4:** K1, (inc1) twice, k1 (6 sts).
**Row 5:** Purl.
**Row 6:** K1, inc1, k2, inc1, k1 (8 sts).
**Row 7:** Purl.
**Row 8:** K1, inc1, k4, inc1, k1 (10 sts).
**Row 9:** Purl.
**Row 10:** K1, inc1, k6, inc1, k1 (12 sts).
Beg with a purl row, work 13 rows in st st.
**Row 24:** Cast off 1 st, knit to end (11 sts).
**Row 25:** Cast off 1 st, purl to end (10 sts).
Place stitch markers on cast-off sts on last
two rows.
Beg with a knit row, work 20 rows in st st.
**Row 46:** Cast on 2 sts, knit to end (12 sts).
**Row 47:** Cast on 2 sts, purl to end (14 sts).
Place stitch markers on cast-on sts on last
two rows.
Beg with a knit row, work 12 rows in st st.
**Row 60:** Cast off 2 sts, knit to end (12 sts).
**Row 61:** Cast off 2 sts, purl to end
(10 sts).
Place stitch markers on cast-off sts on last
two rows.
Beg with a knit row, work 20 rows in st st.
**Row 82:** Cast on 2 sts, knit to end (12 sts).
**Row 83:** Cast on 2 sts, purl to end (14 sts).
Place stitch markers on cast-on sts on last
two rows.
Beg with a knit row, work 8 rows in st st
(place markers at each end of 6th row).
**Row 92:** K1, sl1, k1, psso, knit to last
3 sts, k2tog, k1 (12 sts).
Beg with a purl row, work 7 rows in st st.
**Row 100:** K1, sl1, k1, psso, knit to last
3 sts, k2tog, k1 (10 sts).
Beg with a purl row, work 7 rows in st st.
**Row 108:** K1, sl1, k1, psso, knit to last

3 sts, k2tog, k1 (8 sts).
Beg with a purl row, work 31 rows in st st;
cut yarn and transfer sts to a stitch holder.

## Back neck and head

Join back seam (cast-off edges of right
and left sides of body) using backstitch or
mattress stitch.
Using 3.25mm needles and A, pick up and
knit 30 sts on neck edge (15 sts from each
of sloping edges).
**Row 2:** Purl.
**Row 3:** K1, sl1, k1, psso, k11, turn.
**Row 4:** Purl.
**Row 5:** K12, turn.
**Row 6:** Purl.
**Row 7:** K11, turn.
**Row 8:** Purl.
**Row 9:** K1, sl1, k1, psso, k7, turn.
**Row 10:** Purl.
**Row 11:** K8, turn.
**Row 12:** Purl.
**Row 13:** K7, turn.
**Row 14:** Purl.
**Row 15:** K1, sl1, k1, psso, k3, turn.
**Row 16:** Purl.
**Row 17:** K4, turn.
**Row 18:** Purl.
**Row 19:** K3, turn.
**Row 20:** Purl.
**Row 21:** K1, sl1, k1, psso, knit to end.
**Row 22:** P1, p2tog, p11, turn.
**Row 23:** Knit.
**Row 24:** P12, turn.
**Row 25:** Knit.
**Row 26:** P11, turn.
**Row 27:** Knit.
**Row 28:** P1, p2tog, p7, turn.
**Row 29:** Knit.
**Row 30:** P8, turn.
**Row 31:** Knit.
**Row 32:** P7, turn.
**Row 33:** Knit.

**Row 34:** P1, p2tog, p3, turn.
**Row 35:** Knit.
**Row 36:** P4, turn.
**Row 37:** Knit.
**Row 38:** P3, turn.
**Row 39:** Knit.
**Row 40:** P1, p2tog, purl to end (22 sts).
**Row 41:** Knit.
**Row 42:** Purl.
**Row 43:** (K2, inc1) 3 times, k4, (inc1, k2)
3 times (28 sts).
**Row 44:** Purl.
**Row 45:** (K3, inc1) 3 times, k4, (inc1, k3)
3 times (34 sts).
**Row 46:** Purl.
**Row 47:** (K4, inc1) twice, k14, (inc1, k4)
twice (38 sts).
**Row 48:** Purl.
**Row 49:** K36, turn.
**Row 50:** P34, turn.
**Row 51:** K33, turn.
**Row 52:** P32, turn.
**Row 53:** K31, turn.
**Row 54:** P30, turn.
**Row 55:** K29, turn.
**Row 56:** P28, turn.
**Row 57:** K27, turn.
**Row 58:** P26, turn.
**Row 59:** K25, turn.
**Row 60:** P24, turn.
**Row 61:** K22, turn.
**Row 62:** P20, turn.
**Row 63:** K18, turn.
**Row 64:** P16, turn.
**Row 65:** K14, turn.
**Row 66:** P12, turn.
**Row 67:** K10, turn.
**Row 68:** P8, turn.
**Row 69:** K6, turn.
**Row 70:** P4, turn.
**Row 71:** Knit to end.
Beg with a purl row, work 3 rows in st st.
**Row 75:** (K6, sl1, k1, psso) twice, k6,

*deer*

(k2tog, k6) twice (34 sts).

Beg with a purl row, work 3 rows in st st.

**Row 79:** (K5, sl1, k1, psso) twice, k6, (k2tog, k5) twice (30 sts).

Beg with a purl row, work 3 rows in st st.

**Row 83:** (K4, sl1, k1, psso) twice, k6, (k2tog, k4) twice (26 sts).

Beg with a purl row, work 3 rows in st st.

**Row 87:** (K3, sl1, k1, psso) twice, k6, (k2tog, k3) twice (22 sts).

Beg with a purl row, work 3 rows in st st.

**Row 91:** (K2, sl1, k1, psso) twice, k6, (k2tog, k2) twice (18 sts).

Beg with a purl row, work 5 rows in st st; cut A and join in C. Transfer sts on to two double-pointed needles (9 sts on each), and transfer 8 sts from stitch holder on to a third double-pointed needle. Using fourth double-pointed needle to knit with, and with RS facing, using C and beg at point where C was joined, commence working in rounds for muzzle (26 sts).

## Muzzle

**Rounds 1 and 2:** Knit.

**Round 3:** K3, sl1, k1, psso, k8, k2tog, knit to end of round (24 sts).

**Round 4:** Knit.

**Round 5:** K3, sl1, k1, psso, k6, k2tog, k3, sl1, k1, psso, k4, k2tog (20 sts).

**Round 6:** Knit.

**Round 7:** K3, sl1, k1, psso, k4, k2tog, k3, sl1, k1, psso, k2, k2tog (16 sts).

**Round 8:** K3, sl1, k1, psso, k2, k2tog, k3, sl1, k1, psso, k2tog (12 sts).

**Round 9:** K3, sl1, k1, psso, k2tog, knit to end of round (10 sts).

**Round 10:** K2, sl1, k1, psso, k2tog, knit to end of round (8 sts).

**Round 11:** K1, sl1, k1, psso, k2tog, knit to end of round.

Cut yarn and thread tail through rem 6 sts.

## Ears (make 2)

Using 3.25mm needles and A, cast on 15 sts.

Beg with a purl row, work 5 rows in st st.

**Row 6:** K1, M1, knit to last st, M1, k1.

**Row 7:** Purl.

Rep rows 6 and 7 once more (19 sts).

Beg with a knit row, work 8 rows in st st.

**Row 18:** K6, sl1, k1, psso, k3, k2tog, k6 (17 sts).

**Row 19:** Purl.

**Row 20:** K5, sl1, k1, psso, k3, k2tog, k5 (15 sts).

**Row 21:** Purl.

**Row 22:** K4, sl1, k1, psso, k3, k2tog, k4 (13 sts).

**Row 23:** Purl; cut A and join in B.

**Row 24:** K3, sl1, k1, psso, k3, k2tog, k3 (11 sts).

**Row 25:** Purl.

**Row 26:** K2, sl1, k1, psso, k3, k2tog, k2 (9 sts).

**Row 27:** Purl.

**Row 28:** K1, sl1, k1, psso, k3, k2tog, k1 (7 sts).

**Row 29:** Purl.

**Row 30:** K1, sl1, k1, psso, k1, k2tog, k1 (5 sts).

**Row 31:** Purl.

Cast off.

## Ear linings (make 2)

Using 3.25mm needles and C, cast on 13 sts.

Beg with a purl row, work 5 rows in st st.

**Row 6:** K1, M1, knit to last st, M1, k1.

**Row 7:** Purl.

Rep rows 6 and 7 once more (17 sts).

Beg with a knit row, work 8 rows in st st.

**Row 18:** K5, sl1, k1, psso, k3, k2tog, k5 (15 sts).

**Row 19:** Purl.

**Row 20:** K4, sl1, k1, psso, k3, k2tog, k4 (13 sts).

**Row 21:** Purl.

**Row 22:** K3, sl1, k1, psso, k3, k2tog, k3 (11 sts).

**Row 23:** Purl.

**Row 24:** K2, sl1, k1, psso, k3, k2tog, k2 (9 sts).

**Row 25:** Purl.

**Row 26:** K1, sl1, k1, psso, k3, k2tog, k1 (7 sts).

**Row 27:** Purl.

**Row 28:** K1, sl1, k1, psso, k1, k2tog, k1 (5 sts).

**Row 29:** Purl.

Cast off.

## Tail

Using 3.25mm needles and A, cast on 15 sts.

Beg with a purl row, work 5 rows in st st.

**Row 6:** K1, M1, knit to last st, M1, k1.

**Row 7:** Purl.

Rep rows 6 and 7 once more (19 sts).

Beg with a knit row, work 8 rows in st st.

**Row 18:** K7, sl1, k1, psso, k1, k2tog, k7 (17 sts).

**Row 19:** Purl.

**Row 20:** K6, sl1, k1, psso, k1, k2tog, k6 (15 sts).

**Row 21:** Purl.

**Row 22:** K5, sl1, k1, psso, k1, k2tog, k5 (13 sts).

**Row 23:** Purl.

**Row 24:** K4, sl1, k1, psso, k1, k2tog, k4 (11 sts).

**Row 25:** Purl; cut A and join in B.

**Row 26:** K3, sl1, k1, psso, k1, k2tog, k3 (9 sts).

**Row 27:** Purl.

**Row 28:** K2, sl1, k1, psso, k1, k2tog, k2 (7 sts).

**Row 29:** Purl.

**Row 30:** K1, sl1, k1, psso, k1, k2tog, k1 (5 sts).

**Row 31:** Purl.

**Row 32:** K1, sl1, k2tog, psso, k1 (3 sts).
**Row 33:** Purl.
Cast off.

### Tail lining
Follow instructions for Tail but work in C throughout.

### Hoof bases (make 4)
Using 3.25mm needles and B, cast on 5 sts.
**Row 1 (and each odd-numbered row):** Purl.
**Row 2:** Inc1, k3, inc1 (7 sts).
**Row 4:** Inc1, k5, inc1 (9 sts).
Beg with a purl row, work 5 rows in st st.
**Row 10:** K2tog, k5, k2tog (7 sts).
**Row 12:** K2tog, k3, k2tog.
Cast off rem 5 sts purlwise.

# Making up
### Legs
Stitch remaining four legs to belly, with tops of legs between marked row ends, and making sure that legs correspond with those on left and right sides of body. With right sides together, pin upper part of body, head and legs to belly, matching legs and matching marked row on neck end of belly to place where neck joins back on upper body. Stitch together all round, leaving the base of each leg open and a small opening on one side of head, just above muzzle.

### Body and head
Turn right sides out and stuff body and head, pushing stuffing into tops of legs; add more stuffing up through holes in base of legs. Stitch a hoof base to the base of each leg.

### Eyes and ears
Push eye posts through knitted fabric on either side of head, following the picture of the finished Deer as a guide to placement. Make sure eyes are firmly secured. Thread a tapestry needle with a length of C and use to outline each eye in chain stitch. For the ears, join in pairs, with right sides out and stitch inner ear to outer ear using tails of C and stuffing other yarn tails inside, to provide a little bit of padding. Stitch ears in place. Add more stuffing to head and neck, if necessary, then close the gap in the side seam on the head using mattress stitch.

### Muzzle
Pull up yarn tail at front of muzzle to close gap, then fold the last few rounds of the muzzle upwards and stitch firmly in place. Thread needle with black yarn and embroider nose in satin stitch just above

this point, then embroider three straight stitches to form mouth, with the stitches following the lines of decreases on either side of the muzzle.

### Tail
Place main piece and lining with right sides together, stitch all round in backstitch, leaving the cast-on edges open, then turn right sides out and stitch to back of body, positioning centre of tail at end of back seam.

### Back
Using C, stitch spots across back with Swiss darning. (You may prefer to do this before making up the deer.)

## Did you know?
Fawns have no scent, so predators cannot smell them.

79

Foxes are equally at home in towns as in the countryside. Mostly nocturnal, they hunt for small mammals, birds, reptiles and insects. They also enjoy fruit and vegetables. Foxes are sociable creatures, living in family groups.

# FOX

# Information you'll need

## Finished size

Fox's head and body measure approximately 21in (53cm) in length, and the tail is approximately 10.5in (27cm) long.

## Materials

Sublime Baby Cashmere Merino Silk DK, 75% Merino, 20% Silk, 5% Cashmere (127yd/116m per 50g ball):
3 x 50g balls in shade 338 Foxy (A)
2 x 50g balls in shade 003 Vanilla (B)
Small amount of black DK yarn
Set of four 3.25mm (UK10:US3) double-pointed needles

1 pair of 3.25mm (UK10:US3) needles
Stitch markers
Polyester toy filling
Tapestry needle
2 x ½in (12mm) brown safety eyes

## Tension

24 sts and 32 rows to 4in (10cm), measured over st st using 3.25mm needles and DK yarn. Use larger or smaller needles if necessary to obtain correct tension.

# How to make Fox

## Upper body and head (in one piece)

Using 3.25mm needles and A, cast on 15 sts.

**Row 1 (and every odd-numbered row, unless otherwise stated):** Purl.

**Row 2:** K1, inc1, k5, M1, k1, M1, k5, inc1, k1 (19 sts).

**Row 4:** K1, inc1, k6, M1, k3, M1, k6, inc1, k1 (23 sts).

**Row 6:** K1, inc1, k7, M1, k5, M1, k7, inc1, k1 (27 sts).

**Row 8:** K1, inc1, k8, M1, k7, M1, k8, inc1, k1 (31 sts).

**Row 10:** K1, inc1, k9, M1, k9, M1, k9, inc1, k1 (35 sts).

**Row 12:** K1, inc1, k10, M1, k11, M1, k10, inc1, k1 (39 sts).

**Row 14:** K1, inc1, k11, M1, k13, M1, k11, inc1, k1 (43 sts).

**Row 16:** K1, inc1, k12, M1, k15, M1, k12, inc1, k1 (47 sts).

**Row 18:** K1, inc1, k13, M1, k17, M1, k13, inc1, k1 (51 sts).

**Row 20:** K16, M1, k19, M1, k16 (53 sts).

**Row 21:** Purl.

**Row 22:** K51, turn.

**Row 23:** P49, turn.

**Row 24:** K47, turn.

**Row 25:** P45, turn.

**Row 26:** K43, turn.

**Row 27:** P41, turn.

**Row 28:** K39, turn.

**Row 29:** P37, turn.

**Row 30:** K35, turn.

**Row 31:** P33, turn.

**Row 32:** K31, turn.

**Row 33:** P29, turn.

**Row 34:** K27, turn.

**Row 35:** P25, turn.

**Row 36:** K23, turn.

**Row 37:** P21, turn.

**Row 38:** K19, turn.

**Row 39:** P17, turn.

**Row 40:** K16, turn.

**Row 41:** P15, turn.

**Row 42:** Knit to end.

Beg with a p row, work 21 rows in st st.

**Row 64:** K19, sl1, k1, psso, k11, k2tog, k19 (51 sts).

**Row 66:** K18, sl1, k1, psso, k11, k2tog, k18 (49 sts).

Beg with a p row, work 7 rows in st st.

**Row 74:** K24, turn.

**Row 75:** Purl to end.

**Row 76:** k22, turn.

**Row 77:** Purl to end.

**Row 78:** K20, turn.

**Row 79:** Purl to end.

**Row 80:** K18, turn.

**Row 81:** Purl to end.

**Row 82:** Knit.

**Row 83:** P24, turn.

**Row 84:** Knit to end.

**Row 85:** P22, turn.

**Row 86:** Knit to end.

**Row 87:** P20, turn.

**Row 88:** Knit to end.

**Row 89:** P18, turn.

**Row 90:** Knit to end.

**Row 91:** Purl.

**Row 92:** K1, sl1, k1, psso, k14, sl1, k1, psso, k11, k2tog, k14, k2tog, k1 (45 sts).

Beg with a p row, work 3 rows in st st.

**Row 96:** K1, sl1, k1, psso, k12, sl1, k1, psso, k11, k2tog, k12, k2tog, k1 (41 sts).

Beg with a p row, work 3 rows in st st.

**Row 100:** K1, sl1, k1, psso, k10, sl1, k1, psso, k11, k2tog, k10, k2tog, k1 (37 sts).

**Row 101:** Purl.

**Row 102:** K1, sl1, k1, psso, k8, sl1, k1, psso, k11, k2tog, k8, k2tog, k1 (33 sts).

**Row 103:** Purl.

**Row 104:** K1, sl1, k1, psso, k6, sl1, k1, psso, k11, k2tog, k6, k2tog, k1 (29 sts).

**Row 105:** Purl.

**Row 106:** K1, sl1, k1, psso, k4, sl1, k1, psso, k11, k2tog, k4, k2tog, k1 (25 sts).

**Row 107:** Purl.

**Row 108:** K1, sl1, k1, psso, k2, sl1, k1, psso, k11, k2tog, k2, k2tog, k1 (21 sts).

**Row 109:** Purl.

## Shape head

**Row 1:** K10, turn.

**Row 2:** Purl to end.

**Row 3:** K9, turn.

**Row 4:** Purl to end.

**Row 5:** K8, turn.

**Row 6:** Purl to end.

**Row 7:** K7, turn.

**Row 8:** Purl to end.

**Row 9:** K6, turn.

**Row 10:** Purl to end.

**Row 11:** K5, turn.

**Row 12:** Purl to end.

**Row 13:** Knit all sts.

**Row 14:** P10, turn.

**Row 15:** Knit to end.

**Row 16:** P9, turn.

**Row 17:** Knit to end.

**Row 18:** P8, turn.

**Row 19:** Knit to end.

**Row 20:** P7, turn.

**Row 21:** Knit to end.

**Row 22:** P6, turn.

**Row 23:** Knit to end.

**Row 24:** P5, turn.

**Row 25:** Knit to end.

**Row 26:** Purl all sts.

**Row 27:** K1, inc1, k3, M1, k11, M1, k3, inc1, k1 (25 sts).

**Row 28:** Purl.

**Row 29:** K1, inc1, k5, M1, k11, M1, k5, inc1, k1 (29 sts).

**Row 30:** Purl.

**Row 31:** K1, inc1, k7, M1, k11, M1, k7, inc1, k1 (33 sts).

**Row 32:** Purl.

**Row 33:** K1, inc1, k9, M1, k11, M1, k9, inc1, k1 (37 sts).
**Row 34:** Purl.
**Row 35:** K1, inc1, (k11, M1) twice, k11, inc1, k1 (41 sts).
**Row 36:** Purl.
**Row 37:** K39, turn.
**Row 38:** P37, turn.
**Row 39:** K36, turn.
**Row 40:** P35, turn.
**Row 41:** K34, turn.
**Row 42:** P33, turn.
**Row 43:** K32, turn.
**Row 44:** P31, turn.
**Row 45:** K30, turn.
**Row 46:** P29, turn.
**Row 47:** K28, turn.
**Row 48:** P27, turn.
**Row 49:** K26, turn.
**Row 50:** P25, turn.
**Row 51:** K24, turn.
**Row 52:** P23, turn.
**Row 53:** K22, turn.
**Row 54:** P21, turn.
**Row 55:** K20, turn.
**Row 56:** P19, turn.
**Row 57:** K18, turn.
**Row 58:** P17, turn.
**Row 59:** K16, turn.
**Row 60:** P15, turn.
**Row 61:** K14, turn.
**Row 62:** P13, turn.
**Row 63:** K12, turn.
**Row 64:** P11, turn.
**Row 65:** K10, turn.
**Row 66:** P9, turn.
**Row 67:** Knit to end.
**Row 68:** Purl.

## Shape muzzle
**Row 1:** (K4, sl1, k1, psso) 3 times, k5, (k2tog, k4) 3 times (35 sts).
Beg with a purl row, work 3 rows in st st.

**Row 5:** (K3, sl1, k1, psso) 3 times, k5, (k2tog, k3) 3 times (29 sts).
Beg with a purl row, work 3 rows in st st.
**Row 9:** (K2, sl1, k1, psso) 3 times, k5, (k2tog, k2) 3 times (23 sts).
Beg with a purl row, work 3 rows in st st.
**Row 13:** (K1, sl1, k1, psso) 3 times, k5, (k2tog, k1) 3 times (17 sts).
Beg with a purl row, work 3 rows in st st.
**Row 17:** (sl1, k1, psso) 3 times, k5, (k2tog) 3 times (11 sts).
Beg with a purl row, work 5 rows in st st.
**Row 23:** K1, (sl1, k1, psso) twice, k1, (k2tog) twice, k1 (7 sts).
**Row 24:** Purl.
Cast off.

## Lower body and head
Using 3.25mm needles and B, cast on 13 sts.
**Row 1 (WS):** Purl.
**Row 2:** Knit.
**Row 3:** Purl.
**Row 4:** K1, inc1, k to last 2 sts, inc1, k1.
Rep rows 1–4 four times (23 sts).
Beg with a p row, work 59 rows in st st.
**Row 80:** K1, sl1, k1, psso, k to last 3 sts, k2tog, k1.
**Row 81:** Purl.
Rep rows 80 and 81 once more (19 sts); place a marker on each end of this row.

## Shape head and neck
**Row 1:** Knit.
**Row 2:** Purl.
**Row 3:** K1, sl1, k1, psso, knit to last 3 sts, k2tog, k1.
Beg with a purl row, work 3 rows in st st.

**Row 7:** As row 3 (15 sts).
Beg with a purl row, work 7 rows in st st.
**Row 15:** K1, inc1, k2, M1, k7, M1, k2, inc1, k1 (19 sts).
**Row 16:** Purl.
**Row 17:** K1, inc1, k4, M1, k7, M1, k4, inc1, k1 (23 sts).
**Row 18:** Purl.
**Row 19:** K1, inc1, k6, M1, k7, M1, k6, inc1, k1 (27 sts).
**Row 20:** Purl.
**Row 21:** K1, inc1, k8, M1, k7, M1, k8, inc1, k1 (31 sts).
**Row 22:** Purl.
**Row 23:** K1, inc1, k10, M1, k7, M1, k10, inc1, k1 (35 sts).
**Row 24:** Purl.
**Row 25:** (K3, sl1, k1, psso) 3 times, k5, (k2tog, k3) 3 times (29 sts).
Beg with a purl row, work 7 rows in st st.
**Row 33:** (K2, sl1, k1, psso) 3 times, k5, (k2tog, k2) 3 times (23 sts).
Beg with a purl row, work 7 rows in st st.
**Row 41:** (K1, sl1, k1, psso) 3 times, k5, (k2tog, k1) 3 times (17 sts).
Beg with a purl row, work 7 rows in st st.
**Row 49:** (sl1, k1, psso) 3 times, k5, (k2tog) 3 times (11 sts).
Beg with a purl row, work 5 rows in st st.
**Row 55:** Sl1, k2tog, psso, k5, k3tog (7 sts).
**Row 56:** P2tog, p3, p2tog.
Cast off rem 5 sts.

## Tail

Using set of four 3.25mm double-pointed needles and A, cast on 18 sts and divide these equally between three needles, using the fourth to knit with.
Knit 3 rounds.
**Round 4:** (K5, inc1) 3 times (21 sts).
Knit 5 rounds.
**Round 10:** (K6, inc1) 3 times (24 sts).
Knit 5 rounds.
**Round 16:** (K7, inc1) 3 times (27 sts).
Knit 5 rounds.
**Round 22:** (K8, inc1) 3 times (30 sts).
Knit 5 rounds.
**Round 28:** (K4, inc1) 6 times (36 sts).
Knit 5 rounds.
**Round 34:** (K5, inc1) 6 times (42 sts).
Knit 5 rounds.
**Round 40:** (K6, inc1) 6 times (48 sts).
Knit 54 rounds.
**Round 95:** (K6, k2tog) 6 times (42 sts); cut A and join in B.
Knit 3 rounds.
**Round 99:** (K12, k2tog) 3 times (39 sts).
Knit 3 rounds.
**Round 103:** (K11, k2tog) 3 times (36 sts).
Knit 3 rounds.
**Round 107:** (K10, k2tog) 3 times (33 sts).
Knit 3 rounds.
**Round 111:** (K9, k2tog) 3 times (30 sts).
Knit 3 rounds.
**Round 115:** (K8, k2tog) 3 times (27 sts).
Knit 3 rounds.
**Round 119:** (K7, k2tog) 3 times (24 sts).
Knit 3 rounds.
**Round 123:** (K6, k2tog) 3 times (21 sts).
Knit 3 rounds.
**Round 127:** (K5, k2tog) 3 times (18 sts).
Knit 2 rounds.
**Round 130:** (K1, k2tog) 6 times (12 sts).
Knit 1 round.
**Round 132:** (K2tog) 6 times.
Cut yarn and thread tail through rem 6 sts.

## Back legs (make 2)

Using 3.25mm needles and A, cast on 5 sts.
**Row 1:** Inc1 in each st (10 sts).
**Row 2:** Purl.
**Row 3:** Inc1 in each st (20 sts).
Beg with a purl row, work 15 rows in st st.
**Row 19:** K18, turn.
**Row 20:** P16, turn.
**Row 21:** K15, turn.
**Row 22:** P14, turn.
**Row 23:** K13, turn.
**Row 24:** P12, turn.
**Row 25:** K11, turn.
**Row 26:** P10, turn.
**Row 27:** K9, turn.
**Row 28:** P8, turn.
**Row 29:** K7, turn.
**Row 30:** P6, turn.
**Row 31:** Knit to end.
Beg with a purl row, work 3 rows in st st.
**Row 35:** K2, (inc1, k3) 4 times, inc1, k1 (25 sts).
Beg with a purl row, work 3 rows in st st.
**Row 39:** K2, (inc1, k4) 4 times, inc1, k2 (30 sts).
Beg with a purl row, work 3 rows in st st.
**Row 43:** K1, inc1, knit to last 2 sts, inc1, k1.
**Row 44:** Purl.
Rep rows 43 and 44 twice more (36 sts).
Beg with a knit row, work 4 rows in st st.
**Row 53:** K2, (k2tog, k4) 5 times, k2tog, k2 (30 sts).
**Row 54:** Purl.
**Row 55:** K2, (k2tog, k3) 5 times, k2tog, k1 (24 sts).
**Row 56:** Purl.
**Row 57:** (K2, k2tog) 6 times (18 sts).
**Row 58:** Purl.
**Row 59:** (K1, k2tog) 6 times (12 sts).
**Row 60:** Purl.
**Row 61:** (K2tog) 6 times.
Cut yarn and thread tail through rem 6 sts.

## Front paws/legs (make 2)

Using 3.25mm needles and A, cast on 5 sts and follow pattern for back leg to end of row 3.
Beg with a purl row, work 5 rows in st st.
Follow rows 19–31 from pattern for back leg.
Beg with a purl row, work 3 rows in st st.
**Next row:** K2, inc1, knit to last 3 sts, inc1, k2.
Beg with a purl row, work 5 rows in st st.
Rep last 6 rows four times more (30 sts).
Cast off.

## Ears (make 2)

Using 3.25mm needles and A, cast on 16 sts.
**Row 1 (WS):** Purl.
**Row 2:** Knit
**Row 3:** Purl.
**Row 4:** K2, sl1, k1, psso, k3, (inc1) twice, k3, k2tog, k2.
Rep rows 3 and 4 four times.
**Row 13:** Purl.
**Row 14:** K2, sl1, k1, psso, knit to last 4 sts, k2tog, k2.
Rep rows 13 and 14 three times (8 sts).
**Row 21:** Purl.
**Row 22:** K2, sl1, k1, psso, k2tog, k2 (6 sts).
**Row 23:** Purl.
**Row 24:** K1, sl1, k1, psso, k2tog, k1 (4 sts).
**Row 25:** Purl.
**Row 26:** K1, sl1, k1, psso, k1 (3 sts).
**Row 27:** P3tog; cut yarn and fasten off.

## Ear linings (make 2)

Using 3.25mm needles and B, cast on 14 sts.
**Row 1 (WS):** Purl.
**Row 2:** Knit.
**Row 3:** Purl.
**Row 4:** K2, sl1, k1, psso, k2, (inc1) twice,

k2, k2tog, k2.
Rep rows 3 and 4 four times.
**Row 13:** Purl.
**Row 14:** K2, sl1, k1, psso, knit to last
4 sts, k2tog, k2.
Rep rows 13 and 14 twice (8 sts).
Continue, following instructions for Ears
from rows 21–27.

## Nose
Using 3.25mm needles and black yarn,
cast on 3 sts.
**Row 1 (WS):** Purl.
**Row 2:** K1, inc2, k1 (5 sts).
**Row 3:** Purl.
**Row 4:** (K1, inc1) twice, k1 (7 sts).
**Row 5:** Purl.
**Row 6:** K1, inc1, k3, inc1, k1 (9 sts).
Beg with a purl row, work 3 rows in st st.
**Row 10:** Cast on 6 sts, knit to end (15 sts).
**Row 11:** Cast on 6 sts, purl to end (21 sts).
Beg with a knit row, work 4 rows in st st.
Cast off.

# Making up
## Body and head
With right sides together, stitch the top
body and head to lthe ower body and
head, leaving gaps between marked rows
for leg openings. Turn right sides out. You
will see that the short-row shaping across
the top of the head has created a curve
on either side, like eyebrows. Insert one
eye on each side, just below these curves.
Make sure eyes are firmly secured. Stuff
head. Thread a needle with length of A
and use this to stitch through head, from
behind each eye, to shape head and make
it slightly narrower at this point. Stuff body.

## Legs
Fold each back leg, with right sides
together, and stitch seam in backstitch,
leaving a small opening. Turn right sides

out, stuff, then stitch opening closed.
Stitch top part of each back leg to sides
of body, towards the back end. Stitch side
seams on each front leg, add stuffing,
then stitch top edge of each front leg
to opening in body.

## Ears, nose and tail
Join the ears in pairs, with right sides out,
and stitch inner ear to outer ear using
tails of yarn and stuffing other yarn tails
inside, to provide a bit of padding. For
the nose, with right sides together, stitch
sloping edges to cast-on edges, then sew
short ends together and place this part
underneath pointed end of head. Stitch
whole nose in place all round. Stitch the
tail in place.

fox

**Did you know?**
If foxes have too much
food, they hide it in a hole
to snack on later.

Squirrels like to eat nuts, berries, seeds and wild mushrooms. They bury nuts and seeds to eat in the winter. Grey squirrels are originally from North America but are now common in the UK, where few red squirrels remain.

# SQUIRRELS

**Did you know?**
Squirrels love to munch. They eat their own body weight in food every week.

# Information you'll need

### Finished size
Squirrel measures approximately
11in (28cm) high and the tail is 12in
(30cm) long.

### Materials
Sirdar Country Style DK, 40% Nylon, 30%
Wool, 30% Acrylic (170yd/155m per 50g):
1 x 50g ball each in shades 396 red (A) for
red squirrel, 400 grey (B) for grey squirrel
and 412 white (C)
Sirdar Funky Fox, 100% Polyester
(55yds/50m per 50g ball):
1 x 50g ball each of shades 802 Red Hot
(D) for red squirrel and 806 Alaska (E) for
grey squirrel

Small amount of brown DK yarn
1 pair of 3.25mm (UK10:US3) needles
Set of four 3.25mm (UK10:US3)
double-pointed needles
Stitch markers
Stitch holder
Polyester toy filling
Tapestry needle
4 x ⁵⁄₁₆in (8mm) black safety eyes

### Tension
24 sts and 32 rows to 4in (10cm),
measured over st st using 3.25mm needles
and DK yarn. Use larger or smaller needles
if necessary to obtain correct tension.

# How to make Squirrel

## Belly

Using 3.25mm needles and C, cast on 2 sts.
**Row 1:** Purl.
**Row 2 (RS):** (Inc1) twice (4 sts).
**Row 3:** Purl.
**Row 4:** K1, (inc1) twice, k1 (6 sts).
**Row 5:** Purl.
**Row 6:** K1, inc1, k to last 2 sts, inc1, k1.
Rep rows 5 and 6 six times (20 sts).
Beg with a purl row, work 9 rows in st st.
**Row 28:** Knit all sts; place stitch markers at beg and end of this row.
Beg with a purl row, work a further 19 rows in st st.
**Row 48:** Knit all sts; place stitch markers at beg and end of this row.
**Row 49:** Purl.
**Row 50:** K1, sl1, k1, psso, k to last 3 sts, k2tog, k1.
**Row 51:** Purl.
**Row 52:** Knit.
**Row 53:** Purl.
Rep rows 50–53 twice, then row 50 once more (12 sts).
Beg with a purl row, work 15 rows in st st.
**Row 78:** K1, sl1, k1, psso, k6, k2tog, k1 (10 sts).
**Row 79:** Purl.
**Row 80:** K1, sl1, k1, psso, k4, k2tog, k1 (8 sts).
Beg with a purl row, work 5 rows in st st; transfer sts to a holder, ready to make head.

## Back body and head (in one piece)

Using 3.25mm needles and A (or B), cast on 42 sts.
**Row 1:** Purl.
**Row 2:** K23, turn.
**Row 3:** P4, turn.
**Row 4:** K5, turn.
**Row 5:** P6, turn.
**Row 6:** K7, turn.
**Row 7:** P8, turn.
**Row 8:** K9, turn.
**Row 9:** P10, turn.
**Row 10:** K11, turn.
**Row 11:** P12, turn.
**Row 12:** K13, turn.
**Row 13:** P14, turn.
**Row 14:** K15, turn.
**Row 15:** P16, turn.
**Row 16:** K17, turn.
**Row 17:** P18, turn.
**Row 18:** K19, turn.
**Row 19:** P20, turn.
**Row 20:** K21, turn.
**Row 21:** P22, turn.
**Row 22:** K23, turn.
**Row 23:** P24, turn.
**Row 24:** K25, turn.
**Row 25:** P26, turn.
**Row 26:** K27, turn.
**Row 27:** P28, turn.
**Row 28:** K29, turn.
**Row 29:** P30, turn.
**Row 30:** K31, turn.
**Row 31:** P32, turn.
**Row 32:** K33, turn.
**Row 33:** P34, turn.
**Row 34:** K35, turn.
**Row 35:** P36, turn.
**Row 36:** K37, turn.
**Row 37:** Purl to end.
Beg with a knit row, work 10 rows in st st.
**Row 48:** K15, sl1, k1, psso, k8, k2tog, k15 (40 sts).
**Row 49:** Purl.
**Row 50:** K14, sl1, k1, psso, k8, k2tog, k14 (38 sts).
**Row 51:** Purl.
**Row 52:** K1, sl1, k1, psso, k10, sl1, k1, psso, k8, k2tog, k10, k2tog, k1 (34 sts).
**Row 53:** P11, p2tog tbl, p8, p2tog, p11 (32 sts).

**Row 54:** K30, turn.
**Row 55:** P28, turn.
**Row 56:** K27, turn.
**Row 57:** P26, turn.
**Row 58:** K25, turn.
**Row 59:** P24, turn.
**Row 60:** Knit to end.
**Row 61:** P10, p2tog tbl, p8, p2tog, p10 (30 sts).
**Row 62:** Cast on 17 sts, knit to end (47 sts).
**Row 63:** Cast on 17 sts, purl to end (64 sts).
**Row 64:** K1, M1, k25, sl1, k1, psso, k8, k2tog, k25, M1, k1.
**Row 65:** Purl.
**Row 66:** K26, sl1, k1, psso, k8, k2tog, k26 (62 sts).
**Row 67:** Purl.
**Row 68:** K1, sl1, k1, psso, k to last 3 sts, k2tog, k1 (60 sts).
**Row 69:** P45, turn.
**Row 70:** K30, turn.
**Row 71:** P29, turn.
**Row 72:** K28, turn.
**Row 73:** Purl to end.
**Row 74:** Cast off 21 sts, knit to end (39 sts).
**Row 75:** Cast off 21 sts, purl to end (18 sts).

## Head

**Row 1:** Knit.
**Row 2:** Purl.
**Row 3:** (K2, inc1) 3 times, (inc1, k2) 3 times (24 sts).
**Row 4:** Purl.
**Row 5:** (K3, inc1) 3 times, (inc1, k3) 3 times (30 sts).
**Row 6:** Purl.
**Row 7:** K26, turn.
**Row 8:** P22, turn.
**Row 9:** K20, turn.

**Row 10:** P18, turn.
**Row 11:** K16, turn.
**Row 12:** P14, turn.
**Row 13:** K12, turn.
**Row 14:** P10, turn.
**Row 15:** Knit to end.
**Row 16:** Purl.
Rep rows 7–16 once more.
**Row 27:** (K3, sl1, k1, psso) 3 times, (k2tog, k3) 3 times (24 sts).
**Row 28:** Purl.
**Row 29:** K7, sl1, k1, psso, k6, k2tog, k7 (22 sts).
**Row 30:** Purl.
**Row 31:** K6, sl1, k1, psso, k6, k2tog, k6 (20 sts).
**Row 32:** Purl.
**Row 33:** K5, sl1, k1, psso, k6, k2tog, k5 (18 sts).
**Row 34:** Purl.
**Row 35:** K4, sl1, k1, psso, k6, k2tog, k4 (16 sts).
**Row 36:** Purl.
**Row 37:** K3, sl1, k1, psso, k6, k2tog, k3 (14 sts).
**Row 38:** P2, p2tog, p6, p2togtbl, p2 (12 sts).
Transfer sts to two double-pointed needles – 6 sts on each needle – and place 8 sts from neck end of belly on 3rd double-pointed needle. With RS facing and using fourth needle to knit with, working in rounds, complete front of head as follows:
**Round 1:** K12, sl1, k1, psso, k4, k2tog (18 sts).
**Round 2:** K2, sl1, k1, psso, k6, k2tog, k2, sl1, k1, psso, k2 (15 sts).
**Round 3:** K1, sl1, k1, psso, k5, k2tog, k2, sl1, k1, psso, k1 (12 sts).
**Round 4:** (K2tog) 6 times.
Cut yarn and thread tail through rem 6 sts.

## Left back outer leg

**Row 1:** Using 3.25mm needles and A (or B), with RS of body facing and cast-on edge uppermost, working from right to left, pick up and knit the first 20 sts.
**Row 2:** Purl.
**Row 3:** K18, turn.
**Row 4:** P16, turn.
**Row 5:** K15, turn.
**Row 6:** P14, turn.
**Row 7:** K13, turn.
**Row 8:** P12, turn.
**Row 9:** K11, turn.
**Row 10:** P10, turn.
**Row 11:** K9, turn.
**Row 12:** P8, turn.
**Row 13:** Knit to end.
**Row 14:** P18, turn.
**Row 15:** Knit to end.
**Row 16:** P17, turn.
**Row 17:** Knit to end.
**Row 18:** P16, turn.
**Row 19:** Knit to end.
**Row 20:** P15, turn.
**Row 21:** Knit to end.
**Row 22:** P14, turn.
**Row 23:** Knit to end.
**Row 24:** P13, turn.
**Row 25:** Knit to end.
**Row 26:** Purl.
**Row 27:** Cast off 10 sts, knit to end (10 sts).
**Row 28:** P7, p2tog, p1 (9 sts).
Beg with a knit row, work 7 rows in st st.
**Row 36:** P6, p2tog, p1 (8 sts).
**Row 37:** Knit.
**Row 38:** P5, p2tog, p1 (7 sts).
**Row 39:** Knit.
**Row 40:** P4, p2tog, p1 (6 sts).
**Row 41:** K1, sl1, k1, psso, k3.
Cast off rem 5 sts.

## Right back outer leg

Using 3.25mm needles and yarn A (or B), with RS of back body facing and cast-on edge uppermost, miss next 2 sts after left leg, then pick up and knit 20 sts. Follow instructions for Left back outer leg to end of row 13.
**Row 14:** Purl.
**Row 15:** K18, turn.
**Row 16:** Purl to end.
**Row 17:** K17, turn.
**Row 18:** Purl to end.
**Row 19:** K16, turn.
**Row 20:** Purl to end.
**Row 21:** K15, turn.
**Row 22:** Purl to end.
**Row 23:** K14, turn.
**Row 24:** Purl to end.
**Row 25:** K13, turn.
**Row 26:** Purl to end.
**Row 27:** Knit.
**Row 28:** Cast off 10 sts, purl to end (10 sts).
**Row 29:** K7, k2tog, k1 (9 sts).
Beg with a purl row, work 7 rows in st st.
**Row 37:** K6, k2tog, k1 (8 sts).
**Row 38:** Purl.
**Row 39:** K5, k2tog, k1 (7 sts).
**Row 40:** Purl.
**Row 41:** K4, k2tog, k1 (6 sts).
**Row 42:** P1, p2tog tbl, p3.
Cast off rem 5 sts.

## Right back inner leg

**Row 1:** Using 3.25mm needles and A (or B), with RS of belly facing, starting at end of marked row and working down towards cast-on edge, pick up and knit 20 sts.
**Row 2:** Purl.
**Row 3:** Knit.
**Row 4:** P18, turn.
**Row 5:** Knit.
**Row 6:** P17, turn.

**Row 7:** Knit.
**Row 8:** P16, turn.
**Row 9:** Knit.
**Row 10:** P15, turn.
**Row 11:** Knit.
**Row 12:** P14, turn.
**Row 13:** Knit.
**Row 14:** P13, turn.
**Row 15:** Knit to end.
**Row 16:** Purl.
**Row 17:** Cast off 10 sts, knit to end.
**Row 18:** P7, p2tog, p1 (9 sts).
Beg with a knit row, work 7 rows in st st.
**Row 26:** P6, p2tog, p1 (8 sts).
**Row 27:** Knit.
**Row 28:** P5, p2tog, p1 (7 sts).
**Row 29:** Knit.
**Row 30:** P4, p2tog, p1 (6 sts).
**Row 31:** K1, sl1, k1, psso, k3 (5 sts).
**Row 32:** Purl.
Cast off.

## Left back inner leg

**Row 1:** Using 3.25mm needles and A (or B), with RS of back body facing, miss 2 cast-on sts after top of Right back inner leg then, starting at next st and working towards first st of marked row, pick up and knit 20 sts.
**Row 2:** Purl.
**Row 3:** Knit.
**Row 4:** Purl.
**Row 5:** K18, turn.
**Row 6:** Purl.
**Row 7:** K17, turn.
**Row 8:** Purl.
**Row 9:** K16, turn.
**Row 10:** Purl.
**Row 11:** K15, turn.
**Row 12:** Purl.
**Row 13:** K14, turn.
**Row 14:** Purl.
**Row 15:** K13, turn.
**Row 16:** Purl.

**Row 17:** Knit.
**Row 18:** Cast off 10 sts, purl to end (10 sts).
**Row 19:** K7, k2tog, k1 (9 sts).
Beg with a purl row, work 7 rows in st st.
**Row 27:** K6, k2tog, k1 (8 sts).
**Row 28:** Purl.
**Row 29:** K5, k2tog, k1 (7 sts).
**Row 30:** Purl.
**Row 31:** K4, k2tog, k1 (6 sts).
**Row 32:** P1, p2tog tbl, p3.
Cast off rem 5 sts.

## Left front paw

Using 3.25mm needles and A (or B), cast on 17 sts.
**Row 1:** K15, inc1, k1 (18 sts).
**Row 2:** Purl.
**Row 3:** K1, M1, k to last 2 sts, inc1, k1 (20 sts).
**Row 4:** Purl.
**Row 5:** Knit to last 2 sts, inc1, k1 (21 sts).
**Row 6:** Purl.
**Row 7:** Knit to last 2 sts, inc1, k1 (22 sts).
**Row 8:** Purl.
**Row 9:** K1, sl1, k1, psso, knit to last 2 sts, inc1, k1.
**Row 10:** Purl.
Cast off.

## Right front paw

Using 3.25mm needles and A (or B), cast on 17 sts.
**Row 1:** K1, inc1, knit to end (18 sts).
**Row 2:** Purl.
**Row 3:** K1, inc1, knit to last st, M1, k1 (20 sts).
**Row 4:** Purl.
**Row 5:** K1, inc1, knit to end (21 sts).
**Row 6:** Purl.
**Row 7:** K1, inc1, knit to end (22 sts).
**Row 8:** Purl.
**Row 9:** K1, inc1, knit to last 3 sts, k2tog, k1.

**Row 10:** Purl.
Cast off.

## Ears (make 2)

Using 3.25mm needles and A (or B), cast on 3 sts.
**Row 1 (and each odd-numbered row):** Purl.
**Row 2:** K1, inc1, k1 (4 sts).
**Row 4:** K1, (inc1) twice, k1 (6 sts).
**Row 6:** K2, (inc1) twice, k2 (8 sts).
**Row 8:** K3, (inc1) twice, k3 (10 sts).
Beg with a purl row, work 3 rows in st st.
Cast off.

## Tail

Using 3.25mm needles and D (or E), cast on 24 sts.
Beg with a knit row, work 16 rows in st st.
**Row 17:** K7, inc1, k8, inc1, k7 (26 sts).
Beg with a purl row, work 5 rows in st st.
**Row 23:** (K8, inc1) twice, k8 (28 sts).
Beg with a purl row, work 5 rows in st st.
**Row 29:** K9, inc1, k8, incl, k9 (30 sts).
Beg with a purl row, work 5 rows in st st.
**Row 35:** K10, inc1, k8, incl, k10 (32 sts).
Beg with a purl row, work 5 rows in st st.
**Row 41:** K11, inc1, k8, incl, k11 (34 sts).
Beg with a purl row, work 5 rows in st st.
**Row 47:** K12, inc1, k8, incl, k12 (36 sts).
Beg with a purl row, work 5 rows in st st.
**Row 53:** K13, inc1, k8, incl, k13 (38 sts).
Beg with a purl row, work 13 rows in st st.
**Row 67:** K1, k2tog, knit to last 3 sts, k2tog, k1.
**Row 68:** Purl.
**Row 69:** Knit.
**Row 70:** Purl.
Rep rows 67–70 five times more.
Cast off rem 26 sts.

### Nose

Using 3.25mm needles and brown DK
yarn, cast on 3 sts.
**Row 1:** Purl.
**Row 2:** K1, M1, k1, M1, k1 (5 sts).
**Row 3:** Purl.
**Row 4:** K1, inc1, k1, inc1, k1 (7 sts).
**Row 5:** Purl.
Cast off.

# Making up
### Body

With right sides together, match 2 sts
between back legs on back and belly, then
stitch back legs together all round. Stitch
side seams of belly and back, up to marked
stitches. Join sloping edge of each paw to
belly, beginning at the ends of the marked
row. Stitch front paws together all round.
Turn right sides out.

### Head

Attach the eyes, then stitch one of the side
seams on the head using mattress stitch.
Stuff the body and head firmly but take
care not to overstuff. Stitch the opening
on the head closed, using mattress stitch.

Pheasants are large birds that are found all around the world in fields and on the edges of woodlands. Male pheasants are much larger than the females and have brightly coloured feathers. Pheasants like to eat seeds, berries, fruit and worms.

# PHEASANT

# Information you'll need

### Finished size
Pheasant measures approximately 8in (20cm) long. The head and neck are about 4in (10cm) long and the tail feathers measure 9½in (24cm) long.

### Materials
Manos del Uruguay Silk Blend DK, 70% Merino, 30% Silk (300yd/270m per 100g skein):
1 x 100g skein in shade 6754 Perlitha (brown variegated) (A)
1 x 100g skein in shade 2200 Arabian (dark brown) (B)
1 x 100g skein in shade 2246 Mediterranean (white) (C)
1 x 100g skein in shade 2325 Arctic (blue-green) (D)
1 x 100g skein in shade 2220 Bering (yellow) (E)
1 x 100g skein in shade 2106 Atlantic (red) (F)
Small amount of black DK yarn
Set of four 3.25mm (UK10:US3) double-pointed needles

1 pair of 3.25mm (UK10:US3) needles
2 stitch holders
Polyester toy filling
2 strips of craft foam, approximately 10in (25cm) x ½in (1cm)
Tapestry needle

### Tension
24 sts and 32 rows to 4in (10cm), measured over st st, using 3.25mm needles. Use larger or smaller needles if necessary to obtain correct tension.

*pheasant*

# How to make Pheasant

## Body: right side (in one piece)

Using 3.25mm needles and A, cast on 3 sts.
**Row 1:** Knit.
**Row 2:** Purl.
**Row 3:** (K1, M1) twice, k1 (5 sts).
**Row 4:** Purl.
**Row 5:** K1, M1, k3, M1, k1 (7 sts).
Beg with a purl row, work 3 rows in st st.
**Row 9:** K1, M1, k2, M1, k1, M1, k2, M1, k1 (11 sts).
Beg with a purl row, work 3 rows in st st.
**Row 13:** K1, M1, k4, M1, k1, M1, k4, M1, k1 (15 sts).
Beg with a purl row, work 5 rows in st st.
**Row 19:** K1, M1, k6, M1, k1, M1, k6, M1, k1 (19 sts).
Beg with a purl row, work 5 rows in st st.
**Row 25:** K1, M1, k8, M1, k1, M1, k8, M1, k1 (23 sts).
Beg with a purl row, work 3 rows in st st.
**Row 29:** K1, M1, k21, M1, k1 (25 sts).
Beg with a purl row, work 3 rows in st st.
**Row 33:** K1, M1, k11, M1, k1, M1, k11, M1, k1 (29 sts).
Beg with a purl row, work 3 rows in st st.
**Row 37:** K1, M1, k27, M1, k1 (31 sts).
Beg with a purl row, work 3 rows in st st.
**Row 41:** K29, turn.
**Row 42:** Purl.
**Row 43:** K27, turn.
**Row 44:** Purl.
**Row 45:** K25, turn.
**Row 46:** Purl.
**Row 47:** K23, turn.
**Row 48:** Purl.
**Row 49:** K21, turn.
**Row 50:** Purl.
**Row 51:** K19, turn.
**Row 52:** Purl.
**Row 53:** K17, turn.
**Row 54:** Purl.
**Row 55:** K15, turn.
**Row 56:** Purl.

**Row 57:** K13, turn.
**Row 58:** Purl.
**Row 59:** K11, turn.
**Row 60:** Purl.
**Row 61:** K9, turn.
**Row 62:** Purl.
**Row 63:** K7, turn.
**Row 64:** Purl.
**Row 65:** K10, turn.
**Row 66:** Purl.
**Row 67:** K12, turn.
**Row 68:** Purl.
**Row 69:** K14, turn.
**Row 70:** Purl.
**Row 71:** K16, turn.
**Row 72:** Purl.
**Row 73:** K18, turn.
**Row 74:** Purl.
**Row 75:** K20, turn.
**Row 76:** Purl.
**Row 77:** Knit all sts.
**Row 78:** Purl.
**Row 79:** K2, sl1, k1, psso, k23, k2tog, k2 (29 sts).
Beg with a purl row, work 3 rows in st st.
**Row 83:** K2, sl1, k1, psso, k9, sl1, k2tog, psso, k9, k2tog, k2 (25 sts).
Beg with a purl row, work 3 rows in st st.
**Row 87:** K2, sl1, k1, psso, k17, k2tog, k2 (23 sts).
Beg with a purl row, work 3 rows in st st.
**Row 91:** K2, sl1, k1, psso, k15, k2tog, k2 (21 sts).
Beg with a purl row, work 3 rows in st st.
**Row 95:** K2, sl1, k1, psso, k13, k2tog, k2 (19 sts).
Beg with a purl row, work 3 rows in st st.
**Row 99:** K2, sl1, k1, psso, k4, sl1, k2tog, psso, k4, k2tog, k2 (15 sts).
Beg with a purl row, work 3 rows in st st.
**Row 103:** K2, sl1, k1, psso, k7, k2tog, k2 (13 sts).
**Row 104:** Purl.

**Row 105:** K11, turn.
**Row 106:** Purl.
**Row 107:** K9, turn.
**Row 108:** Purl.
**Row 109:** K8, turn.
**Row 110:** Purl.
**Row 111:** K7, turn.
**Row 112:** Purl.
**Row 113:** K5, turn.
**Row 114:** Purl.
Cut yarn, leaving a tail, and transfer all sts to a stitch holder.

## Body: left side (in one piece)

Using 3.25mm needles and A, cast on 3 sts.
Work as for right side from rows 1–37.
**Row 38:** Purl.
**Row 39:** Knit.
**Row 40:** P29, turn.
**Row 41:** Knit.
**Row 42:** P27, turn.
**Row 43:** Knit.
**Row 44:** P25, turn.
**Row 45:** Knit.
**Row 46:** P23, turn.
**Row 47:** Knit.
**Row 48:** P21, turn.
**Row 49:** Knit.
**Row 50:** P19, turn.
**Row 51:** Knit.
**Row 52:** P17, turn.
**Row 53:** Knit.
**Row 54:** P15, turn.
**Row 57:** Knit.
**Row 58:** P13, turn.
**Row 59:** Knit.
**Row 60:** P11, turn.
**Row 61:** Knit.
**Row 62:** P9, turn.
**Row 63:** Knit.
**Row 64:** P7, turn.
**Row 65:** Knit.

**Row 66:** P10, turn.
**Row 67:** Knit.
**Row 68:** P12, turn.
**Row 69:** Knit.
**Row 70:** P14, turn.
**Row 71:** Knit.
**Row 72:** P16, turn.
**Row 73:** Knit.
**Row 74:** P18, turn.
**Row 75:** Knit.
**Row 76:** P20, turn.
**Row 77:** Knit.
**Row 78:** Purl.
Work as for right side from rows 79–103.
**Row 104:** P11, turn.
**Row 105:** Knit.
**Row 106:** P9, turn.
**Row 107:** Knit.
**Row 108:** P8, turn.
**Row 109:** Knit.
**Row 110:** P7, turn.
**Row 111:** Knit.
**Row 112:** P5, turn.
**Row 113:** Knit.
**Row 114:** Purl.
Cut yarn, leaving a tail, and transfer all sts to a stitch holder.

## Body: underside

Using 3.25mm needles and B, cast on 3 sts.
Beg with a k row, work 4 rows in st st.
**Row 5:** K1, M1, k1, M1, k1 (5 sts).
Beg with a p row, work 7 rows in st st.
**Row 13:** K1, M1, k3, M1, k1 (7 sts).
Beg with a p row, work 9 rows in st st.
**Row 23:** K1, M1, k5, M1, k1 (9 sts).
Beg with a p row, work 11 rows in st st.
**Row 35:** K1, M1, k7, M1, k1 (11 sts).
Beg with a p row, work 13 rows in st st.
**Row 49:** K1, M1, k4, M1, k1, M1, k4, M1, k1 (15 sts).
Beg with a p row, work 7 rows in st st.

**Row 57:** K7, M1, k1, M1, k7 (17 sts).
Beg with a p row, work 25 rows in st st.
**Row 83:** K7, sl1, k2tog, psso, k7 (15 sts).
Beg with a p row, work 3 rows in st st.
**Row 87:** K6, sl1, k2tog, psso, k6 (13 sts).
Beg with a p row, work 3 rows in st st.
**Row 91:** K5, sl1, k2tog, psso, k5 (11 sts).
Beg with a p row, work 3 rows in st st.
**Row 95:** K4, sl1, k2tog, psso, k4 (9 sts).
Beg with a p row, work 3 rows in st st.
**Row 99:** K3, sl1, k2tog, psso, k3 (7 sts).
Beg with a p row, work 3 rows in st st.
**Row 103:** K2, sl1, k2tog, psso, k2 (5 sts).
Beg with a p row, work 5 rows in st st.
**Row 109:** K1, sl1, k2tog, psso, k1 (3 sts).
Beg with a p row, work 5 rows in st st; cut B and join in C.
**Row 115:** K3, then k13 sts from holder for right side, then k13 sts from holder for left side (29 sts); distribute sts between three double-pointed needles, using the fourth to knit with, and commence working in rounds.

## Neck and head

**Round 1:** With RS facing, k2, k2tog, k11, k2tog, k to end of round (27 sts).
**Rounds 2 and 3:** Knit; cut C and join in D. Knit 12 rounds.
**Round 16:** (K2tog, k7) 3 times (24 sts); begin working in short rows.
**Row 1:** K22, turn.
**Row 2:** P20, turn.
**Row 3:** K19, turn.
**Row 4:** P18, turn.
**Row 5:** K17, turn.
**Row 6:** P16, turn.
**Row 7:** K15, turn.
**Row 8:** P14, turn.
**Row 9:** K13, turn.
**Row 10:** P12, turn.
**Row 11:** K11, turn.
**Row 12:** P10, turn.

**Row 13:** K9, turn.
**Row 14:** P8, turn.
**Row 15:** K7, turn.
**Row 16:** P6, turn.
**Row 17:** K5, turn.
**Row 18:** P4, turn.
**Row 19:** K14; do not turn but resume working in rounds.
**Rounds 1–6:** Knit.
**Round 7:** (Sl1, k1, psso, k2) twice, sl1, k1, psso, k4, k2tog, (k2, k2tog) twice (18 sts).
**Rounds 8–10:** Knit.
**Round 11:** (Sl1, k1, psso, k1) twice, sl1, k1, psso, k2, k2tog, (k1, k2tog) twice (12 sts).
**Round 12:** Knit; cut D and rejoin C.
**Round 13:** Knit.
Cast off.

## Beak

Using 3.25mm needles and E, cast on 2 sts.
**Row 1 (WS):** Purl.
**Row 2:** (inc1) twice (4 sts).
**Row 3:** Purl.
**Row 4:** K1, (inc1) twice, k1 (6 sts).
**Row 5:** Purl.
**Row 6:** K1, inc1, k1, M1, k1, inc1, k1 (9 sts).
**Row 7:** Purl.
**Row 8:** (K1, inc1) 4 times, k1 (13 sts).
**Row 9:** Purl.
Cast off.

## Legs (make 2)

Using 3.25mm needles and B, cast on 7 sts.
Beg with a purl row, work 15 rows in st st.
**Row 16:** (K1, M1, k2, M1) twice, k1 (11 sts).
**Row 17:** Purl.
**Row 18:** K1, (M1, k3) 3 times, M1, k1 (15 sts).

**Row 19:** Purl.
Cast off.

## Double claws (make 2)
Using 3.25mm needles and B, cast on
25 sts.
Cast off.

## Single claws (make 2)
Using 3.25mm needles and B, cast on
12 sts.
Cast off.

## Wings (make 4)
Using 3.25mm needles and A, cast on
3 sts.
Beg with a knit row, work 4 rows in st st.
**Row 5 (RS):** K1, M1, k1, M1, k1 (5 sts).
Beg with a p row, work 5 rows in st st.
**Row 11:** (K1, M1) 4 times, k1 (9 sts).
Beg with a p row, work 5 rows in st st.
**Row 17:** K1, M1, k3, M1, k1, M1, k3, M1,
k1 (13 sts).
Beg with a p row, work 5 rows in st st.
**Row 23:** K1, M1, k5, M1, k1, M1, k5, M1,
k1 (17 sts).
Beg with a p row, work 5 rows in st st.
**Row 29:** K1, M1, k7, M1, k1, M1, k7, M1,
k1 (21 sts).
Beg with a p row, work 5 rows in st st.
**Row 35:** K1, sl1, k1, psso, k7, M1, k1,
M1, k7, k2tog, k1.
**Row 36:** Purl.
**Row 37:** Knit.
**Row 38:** Purl.
Rep rows 35–38 twice.
**Row 47:** K8, sl1, k1, psso, k1, k2tog, k8
(19 sts).
Beg with a p row, work 3 rows in st st.
**Row 51:** K7, sl1, k1, psso, k1, k2tog, k7
(17 sts).
**Row 52:** Purl.
**Row 53:** K1, sl1, k1, psso, k3, sl1, k1,
psso, k1, k2tog, k3, k2tog, k1 (13 sts).
**Row 54:** Purl.

**Row 55:** K1, sl1, k1, psso, k7, k2tog, k1
(11 sts).
**Row 56:** Purl.
**Row 57:** K1, sl1, k1, psso, k5, k2tog, k1
(9 sts).
**Row 58:** Purl.
**Row 59:** K1, sl1, k1, psso, k3, k2tog, k1.
Cast off rem 7 sts purlwise.

## Tail feathers (make 2)
Using 3.25mm needles and A, cast on
9 sts.
Beg with a k row, work 70 rows in st st.
**Row 71:** K1, sl1, k1, psso, k3, k2tog, k1
(7 sts).
Beg with a p row, work 7 rows in st st.
**Row 79:** K1, sl1, k1, psso, k1, k2tog, k1
(5 sts).
Beg with a p row, work 5 rows in st st.
**Row 85:** K1, sl1, k2tog, psso, k1 (3 sts).
Beg with a p row, work 3 rows in st st.
**Row 89:** Sl1, k2tog, psso; cut yarn and
fasten off.

## Wattles (make 2)
Using four 3.25mm double-pointed
needles and F, cast on 6 sts and distribute
between three needles.
**Round 1:** Knit.
**Round 2:** (Inc1) 6 times (12 sts).
**Round 3:** (Inc1, k1) 6 times (18 sts).
**Round 4:** (Inc1, k2) 6 times (24 sts).
Cast off.

# Making up
## Body
Join the sides of the body and the
underside together, using mattress stitch.
Leave a small opening at the tail end and
another along one side seam. Inserting the
stuffing through the gap in the side seam,
stuff the body, neck and head firmly but
take care not to overstuff.

## Beak
Fold each side of the beak to the centre
and stitch, then place the cast-off edge
of the beak over the cast-off edge on
the head, overlapping the row of white
stitches slightly, and stitch in place.

## Head
On each wattle, with E, stitch a rosette
of straight stitches, radiating out from
the centre of the wattle, then stitch a
few black stitches in the centre, to form a
beady eye. Stitch one wattle in place on
each side of the head.

## Claws
For the claws, fold a double claw in half
and stitch the end of a single claw to
the fold. Stitch together the cast-on and
cast-off edges on each leg and stitch a
completed claw to the narrower end of
each one, then stitch the wider end of
each leg to the body, about halfway along
the seam on each side. Add a tiny amount
of stuffing, if necessary, to pad out the
top of the leg.

## Wings
For the wings, place two pieces together,
wrong sides out, and join long edges with
a backstitch seam, leaving a small gap in
the seam for turning. Turn right sides out
and close the gap, then stitch the cast-off
edges to side of body.

## Tail feathers
Trim one end of each strip of craft foam,
tapering it to a point. Place one strip on
the wrong side of one of the knitted tail
feathers, bring each long side to the centre
and join using mattress stitch. Do the same
with the other tail feather. Insert the blunt
end of each tail feather into the opening at
the back of the body and stitch in place.

## Crest

Using 3.25mm needles and D, pick up and knit 5 sts across top of head, just behind wattles.

**Row 1:** Purl.
**Row 2:** Knit.
**Row 3:** Purl.
**Row 4:** K1, sl1, k2tog, psso, k1 (3 sts).
**Row 5:** Purl.
Cast off.

### Did you know?
Pheasants originally came from the steamy tropical forests of South-east Asia.

Hedgehogs emerge at night to forage in hedges and undergrowth for worms, snails, mice and frogs to eat. During the day, they curl up into a prickly ball to snooze. Their stiff, sharp spines encourage predators to leave them in peace.

# HEDGEHOG

# Information you'll need

### Finished size
Hedgehog measures approximately 8¼in (21cm) long.

### Materials
Sirdar Funky Fur, 100% Polyester (98yd/90m per 50g ball)
1 x 50g ball in shade 548 Chocolate (A)
Sirdar Click DK, 70% Acrylic, 30% Wool (164yd/150m per 50g ball):
1 x 50g ball in shade 176 Shale (B)
1 x 50g ball in shade 196 Heath (C)
Small amount of black DK yarn (D)
Sirdar Simply Recycled DK, 51% Recycled Cotton, 49% Acrylic (142yd/130m per 50g ball):

1 x 50g ball in shade 15 Camomile (E)
1 pair of 3.25mm (UK10:US3) needles
Set of four 3.25mm (UK10:US3) double-pointed needles
Stitch holder
Polyester toy filling
Tapestry needle
2 x ⁵⁄₁₆in (8mm) black safety eyes

### Tension
24 sts and 32 rows to 4in (10cm), measured over st st, using 3.25mm needles. Use larger or smaller needles if necessary to obtain correct tension.

### Did you know?
As hedgehogs snuffle around the hedges, they make pig-like grunts – hence the name.

# How to make Hedgehog

## Upper body

Using 3.25mm needles and A, cast on
8 sts.
**Row 1 (WS):** Purl.
**Row 2:** (Inc1) 8 times (16 sts).
**Row 3:** Purl.
**Row 4:** (K1, inc1) 8 times (24 sts).
**Row 5:** Purl.
**Row 6:** (K2, inc1) 8 times (32 sts).
**Row 7:** Purl.
**Row 8:** (K3, inc1) 8 times (40 sts).
**Row 9:** Purl.
**Row 10:** (K4, inc1) 8 times (48 sts).
**Row 11:** Purl.
**Row 12:** (K5, inc1) 8 times (56 sts).
Beg with a purl row, work 19 rows in st st.
**Row 32:** K52, turn.
**Row 33:** P48, turn.
**Row 34:** K46, turn.
**Row 35:** P44, turn.
**Row 36:** K42, turn.
**Row 37:** P40, turn.
**Row 38:** K38, turn.
**Row 39:** P36, turn.
**Row 40:** K34, turn.
**Row 41:** P32, turn.
**Row 42:** K30, turn.
**Row 43:** P28, turn.
**Row 44:** K26, turn.
**Row 45:** P24, turn.
**Row 46:** K22, turn.
**Row 47:** P20, turn.
**Row 48:** K18, turn.
**Row 49:** P16, turn.
**Row 50:** Knit to end.
Beg with a purl row, work 3 rows in st st.
**Row 54:** (K5, k2tog) 8 times (48 sts).
**Row 55:** Purl.
**Row 56:** (K4, k2tog) 8 times (40 sts).
**Row 57:** Purl; transfer all sts to a stitch
holder.

## Belly

Using 3.25mm needles and B, cast on
8 sts.
**Row 1 (WS):** Purl.
**Row 2:** (Inc1) 8 times (16 sts).
**Row 3:** Purl.
**Row 4:** K1, inc1, k to last 2 sts, inc1, k1.
Rep rows 3 and 4 seven times more
(32 sts).
Beg with a purl row, work 21 rows in st st;
do not break yarn.

## Snout

Begin working in the round: transfer
stitches on the needle and from the
holder, dividing them between three
double-pointed needles. Put 32 stitches
of B from the belly on one needle and
20 sts from the back (A) on each of the
other two needles. Use the fourth needle
to knit with (72 sts).
**Round 1:** Knit.
**Round 2:** Knit.
**Round 3:** (K3, sl1, k1, psso) twice, k12,
(k2tog, k5) twice, (k4, sl1, k1, psso) twice,
k12, (k2tog, k4) twice (64 sts).
**Round 4:** Knit.
**Round 5:** K7, sl1, k1, psso, k10, k2tog,
k11, sl1, k1, psso, k3, sl1, k1, psso, k14,
k2tog, k3, k2tog, k4 (58 sts).
**Round 6:** Knit.
**Round 7:** K7, sl1, k1, psso, k8, k2tog,
k10, sl1, k1, psso, k3, sl1, k1, psso, k12,
(k2tog, k3) twice (52 sts).
**Round 8:** Knit.
**Round 9:** K7, sl1, k1, psso, k6, k2tog,
k10, sl1, k1, psso, k2, sl1, k1, psso, k10,
k2tog, k2, k2tog, k3 (46 sts).
**Round 10:** Knit.
**Round 11:** K7, sl1, k1, psso, k4, k2tog,
k9, sl1, k1, psso, k2, sl1, k1, psso, k8,
(k2tog, k2) twice (40 sts).

**Round 12:** Knit.
**Round 13:** (K7, sl1, k1, psso, k2, k2tog,
k7) twice (36 sts).
**Round 14:** Knit; cut B and join in C.
**Rounds 15 and 16:** Knit.
Commence working in short rows:
**Row 1:** K19, turn.
**Row 2:** P20, turn.
**Row 3:** K18, turn.
**Row 4:** P16, turn.
**Row 5:** K14, turn.
**Row 6:** P12, turn.
**Row 7:** K33; do not turn but recommence
working in rounds.
**Round 1:** (K4, k2tog) 6 times (30 sts).
**Round 2 and 3:** Knit.
**Round 4:** (K3, k2tog) 6 times (24 sts).
**Round 5:** Knit.
**Round 6:** (K2, k2tog) 6 times (18 sts).
**Round 7:** Knit.
**Round 8:** (K1, k2tog) 6 times (12 sts).
**Round 9:** Knit.
**Round 10:** (K1, k2tog) 4 times; cut C and
join in D.

## Nose

Knit 4 rounds; cut yarn, leaving a tail, and
thread through remaining 8 sts.

## Legs (make 4)

Using 3.25mm needles and B, cast on
4 sts.
**Row 1 (WS):** Purl.
**Row 2:** K1, (inc1) twice, k1 (6 sts).
**Row 3:** Purl.
**Row 4:** K1, inc1, k2, inc1, k1 (8 sts).
**Row 5:** Purl.
**Row 6:** K1, inc1, k4, inc1, k1 (10 sts).
Beg with a purl row, work 7 rows in st st;
cut yarn and join in E.
Beg with a knit row, work 6 rows in st st.

### Claws

Cast off 3 sts, *transfer st from RH to LH needle, cast on 5 sts, cast off 6 sts**; rep from * to ** 3 times more.
Cast off rem 3 sts.

## Making up
### Nose and eyes.
Use the tail of black yarn to neaten the nose, then use it to stuff inside the nose, to create firmness. Insert the eyes into the ridges formed by decreases, just above the colour change on the snout.

### Body and head
Oversew the cast-on edges of the top body and the belly together. Turn the hedgehog inside out and stitch the side seams in backstitch, leaving a small gap in the centre of one of these seams. Turn right sides out and stuff the body and head firmly but take care not to overstuff. Stitch the gap closed.

### Feet and legs
Neaten each claw by oversewing the long edges of each one together, to make them narrower and firmer, then fold in both edges of the foot towards the centre, and stitch the edges together neatly. Leave the top (sloping) edges unstitched. Push a little stuffing into each leg, then stitch the top part of each one to the body, using the picture of the finished hedgehog as a guide to positioning.

Owls have big beady eyes, great for seeing in the dark as they swoop through the woods at night in search of a meal. They have large talons for grabbing their prey and gripping on to branches as they perch in the trees.

# OWL

# Information you'll need

## Finished size

Owl measures approximately 8½in (22cm) high and has a wingspan of 11in (28cm).

## Materials

Sirdar Click DK, 70% Acrylic, 30% Wool (164yd/150m per 50g ball):
1 x 50g ball in shade 167 Peppercorn (A)
Sublime Baby Cashmere Merino Silk DK, 75% Merino Wool, 20% Silk, 5% Cashmere (127yd/116m per 50g ball):
1 x 50g ball in shade 005 Waterlily (B)
1 x 50g ball in shade 303 Buttercup (C)

1 pair of 3.25mm (UK10:US3) needles
Set of four 3.25mm (UK10:US3) double-pointed needles
Polyester toy filling
Tapestry needle
2 x ⅝in (16mm) amber safety eyes

## Tension

24 sts and 32 rows to 4in (10cm), measured over st st, using 3.25mm needles. Use larger or smaller needles if necessary to obtain correct tension.

## How to make Owl

**Body (in one piece)**

Using set of four 3.25mm double-pointed needles and A, cast on 6 sts and divide between three needles, using the fourth needle to knit with.

**Round 1:** Knit.
**Round 2:** Inc1 in each st (12 sts).
**Round 3:** (K1, inc1) 6 times (18 sts).
**Round 4:** (K2, inc1) 6 times (24 sts).
**Round 5:** (K3, inc1) 6 times (30 sts).
**Round 6:** (K4, inc1) 6 times (36 sts).
**Round 7:** (K5, inc1) 6 times (42 sts).
**Round 8:** Knit.
**Round 9:** (K6, inc1) 6 times (48 sts).
**Round 10:** Knit.
**Round 11:** (K7, inc1) 6 times (54 sts).
**Round 12:** Knit.
**Round 13:** (K8, inc1) 6 times (60 sts).
Knit 30 rounds.
**Round 44:** (K8, k2tog) 6 times (54 sts).
**Round 45:** Knit.
**Round 46:** (K7, k2tog) 6 times (48 sts).
**Round 47:** Knit.
**Round 48:** (K6, k2tog) 6 times (42 sts).
**Round 49:** Knit.
**Round 50:** (K5, k2tog) 6 times (36 sts).
**Round 51:** (K4, k2tog) 6 times (30 sts).
**Round 52:** (K3, k2tog) 6 times (24 sts).
Cast off.

### Head

Using set of four 3.25mm double-pointed needles and B, cast on 6 sts and divide between three needles, using the fourth one to knit with.
Follow instructions for body to the end of round 13.
Knit 11 rounds; cut B and join in A.
**Round 25:** (K8, k2tog) 6 times (54 sts).
**Round 26:** Knit.
**Round 27:** (K7, k2tog) 6 times (48 sts).
**Round 28:** Knit.
**Round 29:** (K6, k2tog) 6 times (42 sts).

**Round 30:** (K5, k2tog) 6 times (36 sts).
**Round 31:** (K4, k2tog) 6 times (30 sts).
**Round 32:** (K3, k2tog) 6 times (24 sts).
**Round 33:** (K2, k2tog) 6 times (18 sts).
**Round 34:** (K1, k2tog) 6 times (12 sts).
**Round 35:** (K2tog) 6 times.
Cut yarn and thread tail through rem 6 sts.

## Wings (make 4)

Using 3.25mm needles and A, cast on
3 sts.
Beg with a purl row, work 3 rows in st st.
**Row 4:** K1, inc2, k1 (5 sts).
Beg with a purl row, work 3 rows in st st.
**Row 8:** (K1, inc1) twice, k1 (7 sts).
**Row 9 (and each odd-numbered row):**
Purl.
**Row 10:** K2, inc1, k1, inc1, k2 (9 sts).
**Row 12:** K3, inc1, k1, inc1, k3 (11 sts).
**Row 14:** K4, inc1, k1, inc1, k4 (13 sts).
**Row 16:** K5, inc1, k1, inc1, k5 (15 sts).
**Row 18:** K6, inc1, k1, inc1, k6 (17 sts).
Beg with a purl row, work 9 rows in st st.
**Row 28:** K1, sl1, k1, psso, k11, k2tog, k1
(15 sts).
**Row 30:** K1, sl1, k1, psso, k9, k2tog, k1
(13 sts).
**Row 32:** K1, sl1, k1, psso, k7, k2tog, k1
(11 sts).
**Row 34:** K1, sl1, k1, psso, k5, k2tog, k1
(9 sts).
**Row 36:** K1, sl1, k1, psso, k3, k2tog, k1
(7 sts).
Cast off.

## Neck frill

Using 3.25mm needles and A, cast on 6
sts, using the two-needle (simple cast-on)
method.
**Row 1:** *Cast off 4 sts, transfer st from
right-hand to left-hand needle, cast on
5 sts; rep from * 20 times, cast off 4 sts,
transfer st from right-hand to left-hand
needle; turn (22 sts).

**Row 2:** Inc1 in each st (44 sts).
Cast off.

## Feet (make 2)

Using 3.25mm needles and C, cast on 75
sts, using the two-needle (simple cast-on)
method.
Cast off, knitting each st tbl.

## Beak

Using 3.25mm needles and C, cast on 1 st.
**Row 1:** Inc2 (3 sts).
**Row 2 (and each even-numbered row):**
Purl.
**Row 3:** Inc1 in each st (6 sts).
**Row 5:** (K1 inc1) 3 times (9 sts).
**Row 7:** (K2, inc1) 3 times (12 sts).
**Row 9:** (K3, inc1) 3 times (15 sts).
Cast off purlwise.

## Ear tufts (make 2)

Using 3.25mm needles and A, cast on
11 sts.
**Row 1:** Purl.
**Row 2:** K1, sl1, k1, psso, k1, inc1, k1,
inc1, k2tog, k1.
**Row 3:** Purl.
**Row 4:** K1, sl1, k1, psso, k5, k2tog, k1
(9 sts).
**Row 5:** Purl.
**Row 6:** K1, sl1, k1, psso, inc1, k1, inc1,
k2tog, k1.
**Row 7:** Purl.
**Row 8:** K1, sl1, k1, psso, k3, k2tog, k1
(7 sts).
**Row 9:** Purl.
**Row 10:** K1, sl1, k1, psso, k1, k2tog, k1
(5 sts).
**Row 11:** Purl.
**Row 12:** K1, sl1, k2tog, psso, k1 (3 sts).
**Row 13:** Purl.
**Row 14:** Sl1, k2tog, psso; fasten off.

# Making up
## Head and body

Insert eyes into front of head and secure
firmly. Stuff head by pushing stuffing into
small hole at back of head, then pull up
yarn tail and fasten off neatly to close
gap. Stuff body, then stitch head to neck
opening. Stitch ear tufts in place on either
side of head.

## Wings

Place a pair of wings, right sides together,
and stitch sides with a backstitch seam.
Turn right sides out and oversew top (cast-
off) edges together; repeat with other pair
of wings. Stitch a wing to each side of the
body, near the neck.

## Frill

Run a length of yarn through the straight
edge of the frill, wrap around the neck,
where the head and body join, pull up to
gather, then stitch in place; join short ends
of frill at centre back.

## Feet and beak

Fold each foot strip into three pleats, to
form claws, then oversew edges together,
to hold in place. Stitch feet to base of
body. For the beak, roll into a cone shape
and stitch edges together. Add a few wisps
of stuffing if necessary, then stitch to the
centre front of head.

Owl

Bears are big and burly, but they are agile climbers and strong swimmers. They're also highly intelligent. Most are omnivores, eating meat and plants, and they have excellent senses of smell, sight and hearing to help them find food.

# BEAR

# Information
# you'll need

### Finished size
Bear is approximately 15½in (40cm) tall.

### Materials
Debbie Bliss Rialto DK, 100% Wool (113yd/105m per 50g ball):
2 x 50g balls in shade 37 Earth (A)
1 x 50g ball in shade 02 Ecru (B)
Small amount of black DK yarn
1 pair of 3.25mm (UK10:US3) needles
Stitch markers
Polyester toy filling
Tapestry needle
2 x ½in (12mm) brown safety eyes

### Tension
24 sts and 32 rows to 4in (10cm), measured over st st, using 3.25mm needles. Use larger or smaller needles if necessary to obtain correct tension.

**Did you know?**
Bears don't hibernate but they do sleep for much of the winter.

bear

# How to make Bear

## Right side (leg, body and head)

Using 3.25mm needles and A, cast on 5 sts.

**Row 1 (WS):** Purl.
**Row 2:** (K1, inc1) twice, k1 (7 sts).
Beg with a purl row, work 3 rows in st st.
**Row 6:** K1, inc1, k3, inc1, k1 (9 sts).
Beg with a purl row, work 6 rows in st st.
**Row 13:** P7, turn.
**Row 14:** Knit to end.
**Row 15:** P6, turn.
**Row 16:** Knit to end.
**Row 17:** P5, turn.
**Row 18:** Knit to end.
**Row 19:** P4, turn.
**Row 20:** Knit to end.
**Row 21:** P3, turn.
**Row 22:** Knit to end.
**Row 23:** Purl.
**Row 24:** K1, inc1, knit to last 2 sts, inc1, k1.
Rep rows 23 and 24 once more (13 sts).
**Row 27:** Purl.
**Row 28:** Cast on 6 sts, knit to last 2 sts, inc1, k1 (20 sts).
**Row 29:** Purl.
**Row 30:** Cast on 3 sts, knit to last 2 sts, inc1, k1 (24 sts).
**Row 31:** Purl.
**Row 32:** Cast on 2 sts, knit to last 2 sts, inc1, k1 (27 sts).
**Row 33:** Purl.
**Row 34:** K1, inc1, knit to end (28 sts).
**Row 35:** Purl.
**Row 36:** K1, inc1, knit to last 2 sts, inc1, k1.
**Row 37:** Purl.
Rep rows 36 and 37 three times (36 sts).
**Row 44:** K34, turn.
**Row 45:** Purl to end.
**Row 46:** K32, turn.
**Row 47:** Purl to end.
**Row 48:** K30, turn.

**Row 49:** Purl to end.
**Row 50:** K28, turn.
**Row 51:** Purl to end.
**Row 52:** K25, turn.
**Row 53:** Purl to end.
**Row 54:** K22, turn.
**Row 55:** Purl to end.
**Row 56:** K19, turn.
**Row 57:** Purl to end.
**Row 58:** K1, sl1, k1, psso, knit to last 3 sts, k2tog, k1 (34 sts).
**Row 59:** P32, turn.
**Row 60:** Knit to end.
**Row 61:** P30, turn.
**Row 62:** Knit to end.
**Row 63:** P28, turn.
**Row 64:** Knit to end.
**Row 65:** P26, turn.
**Row 66:** Knit to end.
**Row 67:** P24, turn.
**Row 68:** Knit to end.
**Row 69:** P22, turn.
**Row 70:** Knit to end.
**Row 71:** P20, turn.
**Row 72:** Knit to end.
**Row 73:** P18, turn.
**Row 74:** Knit to end.
**Row 75:** P16, turn.
**Row 76:** Knit to end.
**Row 77:** P14, turn.
**Row 78:** Knit to end.
**Row 79:** P12, turn.
**Row 80:** Knit to end.
**Row 81:** P10, turn.
**Row 82:** Knit to end.
**Row 83:** P8, turn.
**Row 84:** Knit to end.
**Row 85:** P6, turn.
**Row 86:** Knit to end.
**Row 87:** P4, turn.
**Row 88:** Knit to last 3 sts, k2tog, k1 (33 sts).
**Row 89:** Purl.

**Row 90:** K14, sl1, k1, psso, k1, k2tog, knit to end (31 sts).
**Row 91:** Purl.
**Row 92:** K13, sl1, k1, psso, k1, k2tog, knit to end (29 sts).
**Row 93:** Purl.
**Row 94:** K12, sl1, k1, psso, k1, k2tog, knit to end (27 sts).
**Row 95:** Purl.
**Row 96:** K11, sl1, k1, psso, k1, k2tog, knit to end (25 sts).
**Row 97:** Purl.
**Row 98:** Knit to last 3 sts, k2tog, k1 (24 sts).
**Row 99:** P22, turn.
**Row 100:** Knit to end.
**Row 101:** P20, turn.
**Row 102:** Knit to last 3 sts, k2tog, k1 (23 sts).
**Row 103:** P17, turn.
**Row 104:** Knit to end.
**Row 105:** P15, turn.
**Row 106:** Knit to last 3 sts, k2tog, k1 (22 sts).
**Row 107:** P12, turn.
**Row 108:** Knit to end.
**Row 109:** P10, turn.
**Row 110:** Knit to end.
**Row 111:** P8, turn.
**Row 112:** Knit to end.
**Row 113:** P6, turn.
**Row 114:** Knit to end.
**Row 115:** P4, turn.
**Row 116:** Knit to end.
**Row 117:** Purl.
**Row 118:** Knit.
**Row 119:** P20, turn.
**Row 120:** Knit to end.
**Row 121:** P18, turn.
**Row 122:** Knit to end.
**Row 123:** P15, turn.
**Row 124:** Knit to end.
**Row 125:** P12, turn.

**Row 126:** Knit to end.
**Row 127:** P9, turn.
**Row 128:** Knit to end.
**Row 129:** P6, turn.
**Row 130:** Knit to end.
**Row 131:** P3, turn.
**Row 132:** Knit to end.
**Row 133:** Purl.
Mark right end of next row with a stitch marker.
**Row 134:** K1, inc1, knit to end.
**Row 135:** Purl.
Rep rows 134 and 135 five times (28 sts).
**Row 146:** K26, turn.
**Row 147:** Purl to end.
**Row 148:** K23, turn.
**Row 149:** Purl to end.
**Row 150:** K20, turn.
**Row 151:** Purl to end.
**Row 152:** K17, turn.
**Row 153:** Purl to end.
**Row 154:** K14, turn.
**Row 155:** Purl to end.
**Row 156:** K11, turn.
**Row 157:** Purl to end.
**Row 158:** K8, turn.
**Row 159:** Purl to end.
**Row 160:** K5, turn.
**Row 161:** Purl to end, place stitch marker.
**Row 162:** Knit.
**Row 163:** P26, turn.
**Row 164:** Knit to end.
**Row 165:** P24, turn.
**Row 166:** Knit to end.
**Row 167:** P22, turn.
**Row 168:** Knit to end.
**Row 169:** P20, turn.
**Row 170:** Knit to end.
**Row 171:** P18, turn.
**Row 172:** Knit to end.
**Row 173:** P16, turn.
**Row 174:** Knit to end.
**Row 175:** P14, turn.

**Row 176:** Knit to end.
**Row 177:** P11, turn.
**Row 178:** Knit to end.
**Row 179:** P8, turn.
**Row 180:** Knit to end.
**Row 181:** P5, turn.
**Row 182:** Knit to end.
**Row 183:** Purl.
**Row 184:** Knit to last 3 sts, k2tog, k1 (27 sts).
**Row 185:** P23, turn.
**Row 186:** Knit to end.
**Row 187:** P21, turn.
**Row 188:** Knit to last 3 sts, k2tog, k1 (26 sts).
**Row 189:** P18, turn.
**Row 190:** Knit to end.
**Row 191:** P16, turn.
**Row 192:** Knit to last 3 sts, k2tog, k1 (25 sts).
**Row 193:** P13, turn.
**Row 194:** Knit to end.
**Row 195:** P11, turn.
**Row 196:** Knit to last 3 sts, k2tog, k1 (24 sts).
**Row 197:** P8, turn.
**Row 198:** Knit to end.
**Row 199:** Purl.
**Row 200:** K1, sl1, k1, psso, knit to last 3 sts, k2tog, k1.
**Row 201:** Purl.
Rep rows 200 and 201 twice (18 sts).
**Row 206:** (K2, sl1, k1, psso) twice, k2, (k2tog, k2) twice (14 sts).
**Row 207:** Purl.
Cast off.

## Left back inner leg

Using 3.25mm needles and A, cast on 5 sts and follow instructions for right side (leg, body and head) to end of row 58.
Beg with a purl row, work 3 rows in st st.
Cast off.

## Left side (leg, body and head)

Using 3.25mm needles and A, cast on 5 sts.
**Row 1 (WS):** Purl.
**Row 2:** (K1, inc1) twice, k1 (7 sts).
Beg with a purl row, work 3 rows in st st.
**Row 6:** K1, inc1, k3, inc1, k1 (9 sts).
Beg with a purl row, work 5 rows in st st.
**Row 12:** K7, turn.
**Row 13:** Purl to end.
**Row 14:** K6, turn.
**Row 15:** Purl to end.
**Row 16:** K5, turn.
**Row 17:** Purl to end.
**Row 18:** K4, turn.
**Row 19:** Purl to end.
**Row 20:** K3, turn.
**Row 21:** Purl to end.
**Row 22:** Knit.
**Row 23:** Purl.
**Row 24:** K1, inc1, knit to last 2 sts, inc1, k1.
Rep rows 23 and 24 once more (13 sts).
**Row 27:** Cast on 6 sts, purl to end (19 sts).
**Row 28:** K1, inc1, knit to end (20 sts).
**Row 29:** Cast on 3 sts, purl to end (23 sts).
**Row 30:** K1, inc1, knit to end (24 sts).
**Row 31:** Cast on 2 sts, purl to end (26 sts).
**Row 32:** K1, inc1, knit to end (27 sts).
**Row 33:** Purl.
**Row 34:** Knit to last 2 sts, inc1, k1 (28 sts).
**Row 35:** Purl.
**Row 36:** K1, inc1, knit to last 2 sts, inc1, k1.
**Row 37:** Purl.
Rep rows 36 and 37 twice, then row 36 once more (36 sts).

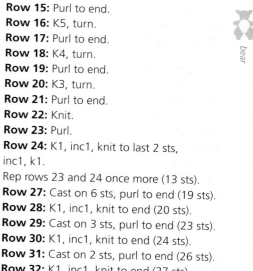

**Row 43:** P34, turn.
**Row 44:** Knit to end.
**Row 45:** P32, turn.
**Row 46:** Knit to end.
**Row 47:** P30, turn.
**Row 48:** Knit to end.
**Row 49:** P28, turn.
**Row 50:** Knit to end.
**Row 51:** P25, turn.
**Row 52:** Knit to end.
**Row 53:** P22, turn.
**Row 54:** Knit to end.
**Row 55:** P19, turn.
**Row 56:** Knit to end.
**Row 57:** Purl.
**Row 58:** K1, sl1, k1, psso, knit to last 3 sts, k2tog, k1 (34 sts).
**Row 59:** Purl.
**Row 60:** K32, turn.
**Row 61:** Purl to end.
**Row 62:** K30, turn.
**Row 63:** Purl to end.
**Row 64:** K28, turn.
**Row 65:** Purl to end.
**Row 66:** K26, turn.

**Row 67:** Purl to end.
**Row 68:** K24, turn.
**Row 69:** Purl to end.
**Row 70:** K22, turn.
**Row 71:** Purl to end.
**Row 72:** K20, turn.
**Row 73:** Purl to end.
**Row 74:** K18, turn.
**Row 75:** Purl to end.
**Row 76:** K16, turn.
**Row 77:** Purl to end.
**Row 78:** K14, turn.
**Row 79:** Purl to end.
**Row 80:** K12, turn.
**Row 81:** Purl to end.
**Row 82:** K10, turn.
**Row 83:** Purl to end.
**Row 84:** K8, turn.
**Row 85:** Purl to end.
**Row 86:** K6, turn.
**Row 87:** Purl to end.
**Row 88:** K1, sl1, k1, psso, k1, turn (33 sts).
**Row 89:** Purl to end.
**Row 90:** K14, sl1, k1, psso, k1, k2tog, knit to end (31 sts).
**Row 91:** Purl.
**Row 92:** K13, sl1, k1, psso, k1, k2tog, knit to end (29 sts).
**Row 93:** Purl.
**Row 94:** K12, sl1, k1, psso, k1, k2tog, knit to end (27 sts).
**Row 95:** Purl.
**Row 96:** K11, sl1, k1, psso, k1, k2tog, knit to end (25 sts).
**Row 97:** Purl.
**Row 98:** K1, sl1, k1, psso, knit to end (24 sts).
**Row 99:** Purl.
**Row 100:** K22, turn.
**Row 101:** Purl to end.
**Row 102:** K20, turn.
**Row 103:** Purl to last 3 sts, p2tog, p1 (23 sts).

**Row 104:** K17, turn.
**Row 105:** Purl to end.
**Row 106:** K15, turn.
**Row 107:** Purl to last 3 sts, p2tog, p1 (22 sts).
**Row 108:** K12, turn.
**Row 109:** Purl to end.
**Row 110:** K10, turn.
**Row 111:** Purl to end.
**Row 112:** K8, turn.
**Row 113:** Purl to end.
**Row 114:** K6, turn.
**Row 115:** Purl to end.
**Row 116:** K4, turn.
**Row 117:** Purl to end.
**Row 118:** K20, turn.
**Row 119:** Purl to end.
**Row 120:** K18, turn.
**Row 121:** Purl to end.
**Row 122:** K15, turn.
**Row 123:** Purl to end.
**Row 124:** K12, turn.
**Row 125:** Purl to end.
**Row 126:** K9, turn.
**Row 127:** Purl to end.
**Row 128:** K6, turn.
**Row 129:** Purl to end.
**Row 130:** K3, turn.
**Row 131:** Purl to end.
**Row 132:** Knit.
**Row 133:** Purl.
Mark left end of next row with a stitch marker.
**Row 134:** Knit to last 2 sts, inc1, k1.
**Row 135:** Purl.
Rep rows 134 and 135 four times and row 134 once more (28 sts).
**Row 145:** P26, turn.
**Row 146:** Knit to end.
**Row 147:** P23, turn.
**Row 148:** Knit to end.
**Row 149:** P20, turn.
**Row 150:** Knit to end.

**Row 151:** P17, turn.
**Row 152:** Knit to end.
**Row 153:** P14, turn.
**Row 154:** Knit to end.
**Row 155:** P11, turn.
**Row 156:** Knit to end.
**Row 157:** P8, turn.
**Row 158:** Knit to end.
**Row 159:** P5, turn.
**Row 160:** Knit to end, place stitch marker.
**Row 161 (and each odd numbered row unless otherwise stated:** Purl to end.
**Row 162:** K26, turn.
**Row 164:** K24, turn.
**Row 166:** K22, turn.
**Row 168:** K20, turn.
**Row 170:** K18, turn.
**Row 172:** K16, turn.
**Row 174:** K14, turn.
**Row 176:** K11, turn.
**Row 178:** K8, turn.
**Row 180:** K5, turn.
**Row 182:** Knit.
**Row 183:** Purl to last 3 sts, p2tog, p1 (27 sts).
**Row 184:** K23, turn.
**Row 185:** Purl to end.
**Row 186:** K21, turn.
**Row 187:** Purl to last 3 sts, p2tog, p1 (26 sts).
**Row 188:** K18, turn.
**Row 189:** Purl to end.
**Row 190:** K16, turn.
**Row 191:** Purl to last 3 sts, p2tog, p1 (25 sts).
**Row 192:** K13, turn.
**Row 193:** Purl to end.
**Row 194:** K11, turn.
**Row 195:** Purl to last 3 sts, p2tog, p1 (24 sts).
**Row 196:** K8, turn.
**Row 197:** Purl to end.
**Row 198:** Knit.

**Row 199:** Purl.
**Row 200:** K1, sl1, k1, psso, knit to last 3 sts, k2tog, k1.
**Row 201:** Purl.
Rep rows 200 and 201 twice (18 sts).
**Row 206:** (K2, sl1, k1, psso) twice, k2, (k2tog, k2) twice (14 sts).
**Row 207:** Purl.
Cast off.

## Right back inner leg
Using 3.25mm needles and A, cast on 5 sts and follow instructions for left side (leg, body and head) to end of row 58. Beg with a purl row, work 3 rows in st st. Cast off.

## Head gusset
Using 3.25mm needles and A, cast on 2 sts.
**Row 1 (WS):** Purl.
**Row 2:** (inc1) twice (4 sts).
**Row 3:** Purl.
**Row 4:** K1, (inc1) twice, k1 (6 sts).
**Row 5:** Purl.
**Row 6:** K1, inc1, knit to last 2 sts, inc1, k1.
Rep rows 5 and 6 four times (16 sts).
Beg with a purl row, work 11 rows in st st.
**Row 26:** K1, sl1, k1, psso, k10, k2tog, k1 (14 sts).
Beg with a purl row, work 3 rows in st st.
**Row 30:** K1, sl1, k1, psso, knit to last 3 sts, k2tog, k1.
**Row 31:** Purl.
Rep rows 30 and 31 twice (8 sts).
Beg with a knit row, work 6 rows in st st.
Cast off.

## Belly
Using 3.25mm needles and B, cast on 5 sts.
Beg with a purl row, work 5 rows in st st.

**Row 6:** K2, M1, k1, M1, k2 (7 sts).
Beg with a purl row, work 3 rows in st st.
**Row 10:** K3, M1, k1, M1, k3 (9 sts).
Beg with a purl row, work 3 rows in st st.
**Row 14:** K4, M1, k1, M1, k4 (11 sts).
Beg with a purl row, work 3 rows in st st.
**Row 18:** K5, M1, k1, M1, k5 (13 sts).
**Row 19 (and each odd-numbered row unless otherwise stated):** Purl.
**Row 20:** K6, M1, k1, M1, k6 (15 sts).
**Row 22:** K7, M1, k1, M1, k7 (17 sts).
**Row 24:** K1, M1, k7, M1, k1, M1, k7, M1, k1 (21 sts).
**Row 26:** K1, M1, k9, M1, k1, M1, k9, M1, k1 (25 sts).
**Row 28:** K1, M1, k11, M1, k1, M1, k11, M1, k1 (29 sts).
**Row 30:** K1, M1, k13, M1, k1, M1, k13, M1, k1 (33 sts).
**Row 32:** K1, M1, k15, M1, k1, M1, k15, M1, k1 (37 sts).
**Row 34:** K1, M1, knit to last st, M1, k1 (39 sts).
**Row 35:** Purl; mark each end of this row with stitch markers.
Beg with a knit row, work 2 rows in st st.
**Row 38:** K1, sl1, k1, psso, knit to last 3 sts, k2tog, k1 (37 sts).
Beg with a purl row, work 3 rows in st st.
**Row 42:** K16, sl1, k1, psso, k1, k2tog, knit to end (35 sts).
**Row 43:** Purl.
**Row 44:** K15, sl1, k1, psso, k1, k2tog, knit to end (33 sts).
**Row 45:** Purl.
**Row 46:** Cast off 2 sts, knit to end.
**Row 47:** Cast off 2 sts, purl to end.
Rep rows 46 and 47 twice more (21 sts).
**Row 52:** K1, sl1, k1, psso, knit to last 3 sts, k2tog, k1.
**Row 53:** Purl.
Rep rows 52 and 53 twice more (15 sts).
Beg with a knit row, work 2 rows in st st.

*bear*

**Row 60:** K1, sl1, k1, psso, knit to last 3 sts, k2tog, k1.
**Row 61:** Purl.
Rep rows 60 and 61 four times (5 sts).
**Row 70:** K1, sl1, k2tog, psso, k1 (3 sts).
**Row 71:** P3tog; cut yarn, leaving a tail, and fasten off.

## Right front paw (outer)
**Row 1:** With right side of right body facing, using 3.25mm needles and A, pick up and knit 19 sts along edge between marked rows.
**Row 2:** Purl.
**Row 3:** Knit.
**Row 4:** Purl.
**Row 5:** K1, sl1, k1, psso, knit to last 3 sts, k2tog, k1 (17 sts).
Rep rows 2–5 once more (15 sts).
Beg with a purl row, work 3 rows in st st.
**Row 13:** K13, turn.
**Row 14:** Purl to end.
**Row 15:** K1, sl1, k1, psso, k9, turn (14 sts).
**Row 16:** Purl to end.
**Row 17:** K10, turn.
**Row 18:** Purl to end.
**Row 19:** K1, sl1, k1, psso, k6, turn (13 sts).
**Row 20:** Purl to end.
**Row 21:** K7, turn.
**Row 22:** Purl to end.
**Row 23:** K1, sl1, k1, psso, k3, turn (12 sts).
**Row 24:** Purl to end.
**Row 25:** K4, turn.
**Row 26:** Purl to end.
**Row 27:** K1, sl1, k1, psso, knit to end (11 sts).
Beg with a purl row, work 5 rows in st st.
**Row 33:** K1, sl1, k1, psso, knit to last 3 sts, k2tog, k1.
**Row 34:** Purl.

Rep rows 33 and 34 twice more.
Cast off rem 5 sts.

## Left front paw (outer)
**Row 1:** With right side of left body facing, using 3.25mm needles and A, pick up and knit 19 sts along edge between marked rows and follow instructions for right front paw (outer) to end of row 9.
Beg with a purl row, work 2 rows in st st.
**Row 12:** P13, turn.
**Row 13:** Knit to end.
**Row 14:** P11, turn.
**Row 15:** Knit to last 3 sts, k2tog, k1 (14 sts).
**Row 16:** P9, turn.
**Row 17:** Knit to end.
**Row 18:** P7, turn.
**Row 19:** Knit to last 3 sts, k2tog, k1 (13 sts).
**Row 20:** P5, turn.
**Row 21:** Knit to end.
**Row 22:** P3, turn.
**Row 23:** Knit to last 3 sts, k2tog, k1 (12 sts).
**Row 24:** Purl.
**Row 25:** Knit to last 3 sts, k2tog, k1 (11 sts).
Beg with a purl row, work 7 rows in st st, then follow instructions for right front paw (outer) from row 33 to end.

## Right front paw (inner)
Using 3.25mm needles and A, cast on 19 sts.
Follow instructions for left front paw (outer) from rows 2–25.
Cut A and join in B, beg with a purl row, work 7 rows in st st, then follow instructions for right front paw (outer) from row 33 to end.

## Left front paw (inner)
Using 3.25mm needles and A, cast on 19 sts.
Follow instructions for right front paw (outer) from rows 2–26.
Cut A and join in B, then continue from row 27 to end.

## Muzzle
Using 3.25mm needles and B, cast on 34 sts.
**Row 1 (WS):** Purl.
**Row 2:** K28, turn.
**Row 3:** P22, turn.
**Row 4:** K20, turn.
**Row 5:** P18, turn.
**Row 6:** K16, turn.
**Row 7:** P14, turn.
**Row 8:** Knit to end.
**Row 9:** Purl.
**Row 10:** K1, (sl1, k1, psso) twice, k24, (k2tog) twice, k1 (30 sts).
**Row 11:** Purl.
**Row 12:** K1, sl1, k1, psso, k10, sl1, k1, psso, k2tog, k10, k2tog, k1 (26 sts).
**Row 13:** Purl.
**Row 14:** (K2, sl1, k1, psso) 3 times, k2, (k2tog, k2) 3 times (20 sts).
**Row 15:** Purl.
**Row 16:** (K1, sl1, k1, psso) 3 times, k2, (k2tog, k1) 3 times (14 sts).
**Row 17:** P5, (p2tog) twice, p5.
Cast off.

## Ears (make 2)
Using 3.25mm needles and A, cast on 12 sts.
**Row 1 (and each odd-numbered row):** Purl.
**Row 2 (RS):** K5, (inc1) twice, k5 (14 sts).
Beg with a purl row, work 7 rows in st st.
**Row 10:** K2, sl1, k1, psso, k6, k2tog, k2 (12 sts).

**Row 12:** K2, sl1, k1, psso, k4, k2tog, k2 (10 sts).
**Row 14:** K1, (sl1, k1, psso) twice, (k2tog) twice, k1 (6 sts).
Cast off purlwise.

## Ear linings (make 2)

Using 3.25mm needles and B, cast on 11 sts.
**Row 1 (and each odd-numbered row):** Purl.
**Row 2 (RS):** K4, inc1, k1, inc1, k4 (13 sts).
Beg with a purl row, work 5 rows in st st.
**Row 8:** K2, sl1, k1, psso, k5, k2tog, k2 (11 sts).
**Row 10:** K2, sl1, k1, psso, k3, k2tog, k2 (9 sts).
**Row 12:** (sl1, k1, psso) twice, k1, (k2tog) twice (5 sts).
Cast off purlwise.

## Foot pads (make 2)

Using 3.25mm needles and B, cast on 5 sts.
**Row 1 (WS):** Purl.
**Row 2:** K2, M1, k1, M1, k2 (7 sts).
**Row 3:** Purl.
**Row 4:** K3, M1, k1, M1, k3 (9 sts).
Beg with a purl row, work 11 rows in st st.
**Row 16:** K2, sl1, k1, psso, k1, k2tog, k2 (7 sts).
**Row 17:** Purl.
**Row 18:** K1, sl1, k1, psso, k1, k2tog, k1 (5 sts).
**Row 19:** Purl.
Cast off.

## Nose

Using 3.25mm needles and black DK yarn, cast on 3 sts.
**Row 1:** Purl.
**Row 2:** Inc1, k1, in1, (5 sts).
**Row 3:** Purl.

**Row 4:** Knit.
**Row 5:** Purl.
**Row 6:** Cast on 3 sts, knit to end (8 sts).
**Row 7:** Cast on 3 sts, purl to end (11 sts).
Beg with a knit row, work 4 rows in st st.
**Row 12:** K2tog, k7, k2tog (9sts).
**Row 13:** Purl.
**Row 14:** K2tog, k5, k2tog (7 sts).
**Row 15:** Purl.
**Row 16:** K2tog, k3, K2tog. Cast off rem 5 sts purlwise.

# Making up
## Body and head

Line up cast-off edges of each side piece, with cast-off edge of head gusset, positioning head gusset between the two side pieces; pin, then stitch sides of gusset to head. Continue stitching back seam.

## Paws and legs

Stitch inner front paws in position at sides of belly. Stitch inner back legs in position between cast on edge and marked rows on belly, then with right sides facing, stitch belly to back.
When stitching seams on back legs, leave base of leg open and insert foot pads, matching centre of cast-on edge of foot pad to leg seam, and sew edges together in backstitch.

## Face

Turn right sides out and stuff the body and head firmly but take care not to overstuff. Insert eyes close to open edge of head, and secure in place, then stitch seam on

muzzle, stuff and stitch cast-on edge of muzzle to cast-off edge of head. Stitch the ear linings to the ears and stitch cast-on edge to head on each side. Stitch nose seams by stitching extra three cast-on stitches to side edges at base of nose, then after adding a little stuffing, if necessary, stitch to front of muzzle. Using black yarn, embroider a line of chain stitch from nose, down seamline on muzzle.

## Claws

Embroider lines of chain stitch on each paw, to represent claws.

**Did you know?**
Bears walk flat-footed, which enables them to walk upright.

The raccoon is a nocturnal creature, with a distinctive bushy ringed tail. Best-known is the North American raccoon, with its black mask across the eyes that makes it look like a superhero. Raccoons are intelligent animals that have adapted to living in urban areas.

# RACCOON

**Did you know?**
A raccoon's tail can make up half of its length.

# Information you'll need

### Finished size

Raccoon measures approximately 17in (44cm) from the tip of the nose to the base of the tail; the tail is 12in (30cm) long.

### Materials

King Cole Baby Alpaca DK, 100% Alpaca (110yd/100m per 50g ball):
2 x 50g balls in shade 502 Grey (A)
1 x 50g ball each in shades 503 Charcoal (B), 501 Fawn (C) and 504 Koala (D)
King Cole Merino Blend DK, 100% Wool (123yd/112m per 50g ball):

1 x 50g ball in shade 46 Aran (E)
Small amount of black DK yarn
1 pair of 3.25mm (UK10:US3) needles
Polyester toy filling
Tapestry needle
2 x ⁵⁄₁₆in (8mm) black safety eyes
Scraps of wool or viscose felt in grey

### Tension

24 sts and 32 rows to 4in (10cm), measured over st st using 3.25mm needles and DK yarn. Use larger or smaller needles if necessary to obtain correct tension.

# How to make Raccoon

## Left side

### Front leg

*Using 3.25mm needles and A, cast on 8 sts.

Beg with a purl row, work 5 rows in st st.

**Row 6:** K1, M1, knit to last st, M1, k1.

Rep rows 1–6 four times more (18 sts).

**Row 31:** Purl.**

Cut yarn and leave sts on a holder.

### Back leg

Follow pattern for front leg from * to **; do not cut yarn.

### Left body

**Row 1:** K1, M1, k16, M1, k1, cast on 8 sts, then working across stitches from holder (front leg): k1, M1, k16, M1, k1 (48 sts).

Beg with a purl row, work 5 rows in st st.

**Row 7:** K1, M1, knit to last st, M1, k1.

Rep rows 2–7 once more (52 sts).

Beg with a purl row, work 5 rows in st st.

**Row 19:** Knit to last st, M1, k1.

Beg with a purl row, work 5 rows in st st.

**Row 25:** As row 19 (54 sts).

**Row 26:** Purl.

**Row 27:** K1, sl1, k1, psso, knit to last 3 sts, k2tog, k1.

**Row 28:** Purl.

**Row 29:** Knit to last 3 sts, k2tog, k1.

**Row 30:** Purl.

Rep rows 27–30 twice more.

Cast off rem 45 sts.

## Right side

Follow instructions for Left side to end of row 18 (note that legs will be reversed: the first leg worked will become the back leg and the second the front leg).

**Row 19:** K1, M1, knit to end.

Beg with a purl row, work 5 rows in st st.

**Row 25:** As row 19 (54 sts).

**Row 26:** Purl.

**Row 27:** K1, sl1, k1, psso, knit to last 3 sts, k2tog, k1.

**Row 28:** Purl.

**Row 29:** K1, sl1, k1, psso, knit to end.

**Row 30:** Purl.

Rep rows 27–30 twice more.

Cast off rem 45 sts.

## Head

Stitch back seam on body.

**Row 1:** With right side facing and neck end of body uppermost, using 3.25mm needles and A, pick up and knit 32 sts along neck edge (16 from each side).

**Row 2:** Purl.

**Row 3:** K1, inc1, knit to last 2 sts, inc1, k1 (34 sts).

Beg with a purl row, work 3 rows in st st.

**Row 7:** K15, inc1, k2, inc1, knit to end (36 sts).

**Row 8:** Purl.

**Row 9:** K34, turn.

**Row 10:** P32, turn.

**Row 11:** K31, turn.

**Row 12:** P30, turn.

**Row 13:** K29, turn.

**Row 14:** P28, turn.

**Row 15:** K27, turn.

**Row 16:** P26, turn.

**Row 17:** K25, turn.

**Row 18:** P24, turn.

**Row 19:** K23, turn.

**Row 20:** P22, turn.

**Row 21:** K21, turn.

**Row 22:** P20, turn.

**Row 23:** Knit to end.

Beg with a purl row, work 11 rows in st st; cut A and join in E.

Beg with a knit row, work 8 rows in st st; cut E and join in B.

**Row 43:** K1, sl1, k1, psso, k14, turn (35 sts).

**Row 44:** Purl to end.

**Row 45:** K1, sl1, k1, psso, k11, turn (34 sts).

**Row 46:** Purl to end.

**Row 47:** K1, sl1, k1, psso, k8, turn (33 sts).

**Row 48:** Purl to end.

**Did you know?**
Raccoons can easily survive a fall of 40 feet (12m).

**Row 49:** K1, sl1, k1, psso, k5, turn
(32 sts).
**Row 50:** Purl to end.
**Row 51:** Knit to last 3 sts, k2tog, k1
(31 sts).
**Row 52:** P16, turn.
**Row 53:** Knit to last 3 sts, k2tog, k1
(30 sts).
**Row 54:** P13, turn.
**Row 55:** Knit to last 3 sts, k2tog, k1
(29 sts).
**Row 56:** P10, turn.
**Row 57:** Knit to last 3 sts, k2tog, k1
(28 sts).
**Row 58:** P7, turn.
**Row 59:** Knit to last 3 sts, k2tog, k1
(26 sts).
**Row 60:** Purl.
**Row 61:** K1, sl1, k1, psso, k7, sl1, k1,
psso, k2, k2tog, k7, k2tog, k1 (22 sts).
**Row 62:** Purl; cut yarn B and join in E.
**Row 63:** Knit.
**Row 64:** Purl.
**Row 65:** K1, sl1, k1, psso, knit to last
3 sts, k2tog, k1.
**Row 66:** Purl.
Rep rows 65 and 66 three times (14 sts).
**Row 73:** K1, sl1, k1, psso, knit to last
3 sts, k2tog, k1 (12 sts).
**Row 74:** Purl.
Rep rows 73 and 74 three times.
Cast off rem 6 sts.

## Inner legs (make 4)

Using 3.25mm needles and A, cast on
8 sts.
Beg with a purl row, work 5 rows in st st.
**Row 6:** K1, M1, knit to last st, M1, k1.
Rep rows 1–6 four times more (18 sts).
**Row 31:** Purl.
Cast off.

## Belly, neck and lower head

Using 3.25mm needles and A, cast on
2 sts.
**Row 1 (and each odd-numbered row,
unless otherwise stated):** Purl.
**Row 2:** (Inc1) twice (4 sts).
**Row 4:** K1, (inc1) twice, k1 (6 sts).
**Row 6:** K1, inc1, k2, inc1, k1 (8 sts).
**Row 8:** K1, inc1, k4, inc1, k1 (10 sts).
**Row 10:** K1, inc1, k6, inc1, k1 (12 sts).
**Row 12:** K1, inc1, k8, inc1, k1 (14 sts).
**Row 14:** K1, inc1, k10, inc1, k1 (16 sts).
Beg with a purl row, work 11 rows in st st.
**Row 26:** Cast off 2 sts, knit to end
(14 sts).
**Row 27:** Cast off 2 sts, purl to end
(12 sts).
Beg with a knit row, work 20 rows in st st.
**Row 48:** Cast on 2 sts, knit to end (14 sts).
**Row 49:** Cast on 2 sts, purl to end (16 sts).
Beg with a knit row, work 12 rows in st st.
**Row 62:** Cast off 2 sts, knit to end (14 sts).
**Row 63:** Cast off 2 sts, purl to end
(12 sts).
Beg with a knit row, work 20 rows in st st.
**Row 84:** Cast on 2 sts, knit to end (14 sts).
**Row 85:** Cast on 2 sts, purl to end (16 sts).
Beg with a knit row, work 22 rows in
st st; place a stitch marker at each end
of last row.

## Lower neck and head

**Row 1:** Knit
**Row 2:** Purl.
**Row 3:** K1, inc1, knit to last 2 sts,
inc1, k1.
**Row 4:** Purl.
Rep rows 1–4 four times (26 sts).
**Row 21:** Knit.
**Row 22:** Purl.
**Row 23:** K1, sl1, k1, psso, knit to last 3 sts,
k2tog, k1.
**Row 24:** Purl.

Rep rows 21–24 three times (18 sts); cut A
and join in E.
**Row 37:** K1, sl1, k1, psso, knit to last 3 sts,
k2tog, k1.
**Row 38:** Purl.
Rep rows 37 and 38 until 4 sts rem.
Beg with a knit row, work 3 rows in st st.
Cast off purlwise.

## Head stripe

Using 3.25mm needles and A, cast on
5 sts.
Beg with a purl row, work 9 rows in st st.
**Row 10:** K2, M1, k1, M1, k2 (7 sts).
**Row 11:** Purl.
**Row 12:** K2, M1, k3, M1, k2 (9 sts).
**Row 13:** Purl.
**Row 14:** K2, M1, k5, M1, k2 (11 sts).
Beg with a purl row, work 3 rows in st st.
**Row 18:** K1, sl1, k1, psso, k5, k2tog, k1
(9 sts).
**Row 19:** Purl.
**Row 20:** K1, sl1, k1, psso, k3, k2tog, k1
(7 sts).
**Row 21:** Purl.
**Row 22:** K1, sl1, k1, psso, k1, k2tog, k1
(5 sts).
Beg with a purl row, work 9 rows in st st.
Cast off.

## Ear linings (make 2)

Using 3.25mm needles and B, cast on
4 sts.
**\*Row 1:** Purl.
**Row 2:** K1, (inc1) twice, k1 (6 sts).
**Row 3:** Purl.
**Row 4:** K2, (inc1) twice, k2 (8 sts).
**Row 5:** Purl.
**Row 6:** K3, (inc1) twice, k3 (10 sts).
**Row 7:** Purl.
**Row 8:** K4, (inc1) twice, k4 (12 sts).
Beg with a purl row, work 11 rows in st st.
Cast off.\*\*

raccoon

## Ears (make 2)

Using 3.25mm needles and A, cast on 4 sts.
Follow instructions for ear linings from * to
**

## Edging

**Row 1:** With RS facing, join C to last st of
cast-off row, then pick up and knit 13 sts
up sloping edge, 4 sts on cast-on row,
13 sts down other edge (30 sts).
**Row 2:** K14, (inc1) twice, k14 (32 sts).
**Row 3:** K15, (inc1) twice, k15 (34 sts).
**Row 4:** K16, (inc1) twice, k16 (36 sts).
**Row 5:** K17, (inc1) twice, k17 (38 sts).
Cast off.

## Nose

Using 3.25mm needles and black yarn,
cast on 3 sts.
**Row 1:** (inc1) 3 times (6 sts).
**Row 2:** (K1, inc1) 3 times (9 sts).
**Row 3:** (K2, inc1) 3 times (12 sts).
**Row 4:** (K3, inc1) 3 times (15 sts).
Knit 3 rows.
Cast off.

## Tail

Using 3.25mm needles and B, cast on
30 sts.
**Row 1:** Purl.
**Row 2:** K24, turn.
**Row 3:** P18, turn.
**Row 4:** K16, turn.
**Row 5:** P14, turn.
**Row 6:** K12, turn.
**Row 7:** P10, turn.
**Row 8:** Knit to end.
**Row 9:** Purl; do not cut B but join in C.
Beg with a knit row, using C, work 8 rows
in st st.
Beg with a knit row, using B, work 6 rows
in st st.
Beg with a knit row, using C, work 8 rows
in st st.

Beg with a knit row, using B, work 4 rows
in st st.
**Row 36:** Using B, k12, sl1, k1, psso, k2,
k2tog, k12 (28 sts).
**Row 37:** Purl.
Beg with a knit row, using C, work 4 rows
in st st.
**Row 42:** Using C, k11, sl1, k1, psso, k2,
k2tog, k11 (26 sts).
Beg with a purl row, still using yarn C,
work 3 rows in st st.
Beg with a knit row, using yarn B, work
4 rows in st st.
**Row 50:** Using B, k10, sl1, k1, psso, k2,
k2tog, k10 (24 sts).
**Row 51:** Purl.
Beg with a knit row, using C, work 4 rows
in st st.
**Row 56:** Using C, k9, sl1, k1, psso, k2,
k2tog, k9 (22 sts).
Beg with a purl row, still using C, work
3 rows in st st.
Beg with a knit row, using B, work 4 rows
in st st.
**Row 64:** Using B, k8, sl1, k1, psso, k2,
k2tog, k8 (20 sts).
**Row 65:** Purl.
Beg with a knit row, using C, work 4 rows
in st st.
**Row 70:** Using C, k7, sl1, k1, psso, k2,
k2tog, k7 (18 sts).
Beg with a purl row, still using C, work
3 rows in st st.
Beg with a knit row, using B, work 4 rows
in st st.
**Row 78:** Using B, k6, sl1, k1, psso, k2,
k2tog, k6 (16 sts).
**Row 79:** Purl.
Beg with a knit row, using C, work 4 rows
in st st.
**Row 84:** Using C, k5, sl1, k1, psso, k2,
k2tog, k5 (14 sts).
Beg with a purl row, still using C, work

3 rows in st st; cut C.
Beg with a knit row, using B, work 6 rows
in st st.
Cast off.

## Front feet (make 2)
### Claws

*Using two 3.25mm double-pointed
needles and D, cast on 2 sts.
**Row 1:** K2; do not turn but slide sts to
other end of needle.
Rep row 1 nine times, cut yarn, leaving a
tail, and transfer sts to a spare needle.**
Rep from * to ** four times but do not cut
yarn after fifth claw.

### Foot

**Row 1:** Knit across all stitches on holder
(10 sts).
**Row 2:** Purl.
**Row 3:** Cast on 2 sts, k to end (12 sts).
**Row 4:** Cast on 2 sts, p to end (14 sts).
**Row 5:** (Inc1) twice, k to last 2 sts, (inc1)
twice (18 sts).
Beg with a purl row, work 3 rows in st st.
Cast off.

## Back feet (make 2)

Follow instructions given for front foot, for
claws and foot to end of row 5.
Beg with a purl row, work 5 rows in st st.
**Row 11:** K16, turn.
**Row 12:** P14, turn.
**Row 13:** K12, turn.
**Row 14:** P10, turn.
**Row 15:** K8, turn.
**Row 16:** P6, turn.
**Row 17:** K4, turn.
**Row 18:** P2, turn.
**Row 19:** Knit to end.
Beg with a purl row, work 5 rows in st st.
Cast off.

# Making up

## Head

Stitch side seams on head, leaving small opening at front of snout. Pin head stripe in position, matching cast-on edge to top of horizontal stripes on face and cast-off edge at front opening. If stripe is too long, tuck excess into this opening, where it will be hidden by nose. Stitch stripe in place.

## Eyes and nose

Cut two circles of grey felt, about ½in (15mm) in diameter, and snip a small hole in the centre of each. Place one on either side of stripe along the colour join on the horizontal stripes, using picture of finished raccoon as a guide. Insert one eye through the centre of each circle, then through the knitted fabric, and secure firmly in place. Stitch seam on nose and stitch to front of snout.

## Legs

Stitch tops of inner legs to indentations along long edges of belly. Place top and underside, right sides together and stitch all round in backstitch, leaving an opening in one side seam, between tops of legs, and leaving lower end of each leg open. Turn right sides out through the gap in the side seam.

## Body and head

Stuff the body and head firmly but take care not to overstuff. Stitch opening in side seam closed, using mattress stitch. Place an ear lining on each ear, right sides out, and oversew in place. Stitch cast-on edges of ears to head.

## Feet

On the front feet, use the tails of yarn to neaten the claws, to stitch the gap closed at the base of the claws and to stitch side seam. Push the cast-off edge of each front foot into the opening at the base of each front leg (adding a little stuffing to front legs before doing so, if necessary), and stitch in place. Do the same with the back feet.

## Tail

Fold tail in half lengthways, with right sides together, and stitch the long edges together, leaving the base (cast-on edge) open. Turn right sides out, stuff and stitch to back of body.

## Did you know?

Raccoons are excellent swimmers and are happy to make dens in riverbanks.

Chipmunks are small, striped rodents with furry tails. They scamper along the ground and up trees to forage for nuts, berries and seeds, which they store in their large cheek pouches. At night, chipmunks sleep in burrows or trees.

# CHIPMUNK

# Information you'll need

## Finished size
Chipmunk is 8¼in (21cm) long, not including the tail, which measures 6½in (17cm) long.

## Materials
King Cole Merino Blend DK, 100% Wool (123yd/112m per 50g ball):
1 x 50g ball in shade 857 Bark (A)
1 x 50g ball in shade 48 Black (B)
1 x 50g ball in shade 1 White (C)
King Cole Moments, 100% Polyester (98yd/90m per 50g ball):
1 x 50g ball in shade 474 Black (D)
1 pair of 3.25mm (UK10:US3) needles
1 pair of 4mm (UK8:US6) needles
2 or 3 safety pins or small stitch holders
Polyester toy filling
Tapestry needle
Two ⅓in (8mm) black safety eyes

## Tension
24 sts and 32 rows to 4in (10cm), measured over st st, using 3.25mm needles. Use larger or smaller needles if necessary to obtain correct tension.

# How to make Chipmunk

## Body

Using 3.25mm needles and A, cast on 18 sts.

**Row 1 (RS):** Inc1 in each st (36 sts).

Beg with a purl row, work 11 rows in st st. Divide for right side.

**Row 1:** K10, turn and leave rem sts on a safety pin or stitch holder.

Beg with a purl row, work 27 rows in st st on these 10 sts.

**Row 29:** K1, sl1, k1, psso, k to end.

**Row 30:** Purl.

Rep rows 29 and 30 three times (6 sts).

**Row 37:** Knit.

**Row 38:** Purl.

Cut yarn; do not cast off but leave sts on a safety pin.

## Centre back

**Row 1:** Rejoin yarn to sts on holder, k16, turn and leave rem 10 sts on holder.

**Row 2:** Purl.

**Row 3:** K1, sl1, k1, psso, k10, k2tog, k1 (14 sts).

**Row 4:** Purl.

**Row 5:** K11, turn.

**Row 6:** P8, turn.

**Row 7:** K7, turn.

**Row 8:** P6, turn.

**Row 9:** K to end.

Beg with a purl row, work 25 rows in st st.

**Row 35:** K1, inc1, k1, k to last 2 sts, inc1, k1.

**Row 36:** Purl.

Rep rows 35 and 36 twice more.

Cut yarn; do not cast off but leave sts on a safety pin.

## Left side

Rejoin yarn to rem 10 sts from stitch holder. Beg with a knit row, work 28 rows in st st.

**Row 29:** K7, k2tog, k1 (9 sts).

**Row 30:** Purl.

**Row 31:** K6, k2tog, k1 (8 sts).

**Row 32:** Purl.

**Row 33:** K5, k2tog, k1 (7 sts).

**Row 34:** Purl.

**Row 35:** K4, k2tog, k1 (6 sts).

Beg with a purl row, work 3 rows in st st. Cut yarn; do not cast off but leave sts on a safety pin.

## Head

Rejoin A to 6 sts from the safety pin for the right side.

**Row 1:** K6, then knit 20 sts from centre, then 6 sts from left side (32 sts).

**Row 2:** Purl.

**Row 3:** (K3, sl1, k1, psso) 3 times, k2, (k2tog, k3) 3 times (26 sts).

**Row 4:** Purl.

**Row 5:** K2, sl1, k1, psso, k18 , k2tog, k2 (24 sts).

**Row 6:** Purl.

**Row 7:** K20, turn.

**Row 8:** P16, turn.

**Row 9:** K14, turn.

**Row 10:** P12, turn.

**Row 11:** K10, turn.

**Row 12:** P8, turn.

**Row 13:** K6, turn.

**Row 14:** P4, turn.

**Row 15:** K to end.

**Row 16:** Purl.

**Row 17:** K8, sl1, k1, psso, k4, k2tog, k8 (22 sts).

**Row 18:** Purl.

**Row 19:** K7, sl1, k1, psso, k4, k2tog, k7 (20 sts).

**Row 20:** Purl.

**Row 21:** K6, sl1, k1, psso, k4, k2tog, k6 (18 sts).

**Row 22:** Purl.

**Row 23:** K5, sl1, k1, psso, k4, k2tog, k5 (16 sts).

**Row 24:** Purl.

**Row 25:** K4, sl1, k1, psso, k4, k2tog, k4 (14 sts).

**Row 26:** Purl.

**Row 27:** K3, sl1, k1, psso, k4, k2tog, k3 (12 sts).

**Row 28:** Purl.

**Row 29:** (K1, sl1, k1, psso) twice, (k2tog, k1) twice (8 sts).

**Row 30:** Purl.

**Row 31:** (Sl1, k1, psso) twice, (k2tog) twice (4 sts).

**Row 32:** (P2tog) twice (2 sts).

**Row 33:** K2tog; cut yarn and fasten off.

## Side stripes (make 2)

Using 3.25mm needles and B, cast on 28 sts.

**Row 1:** P23, turn.

**Row 2:** K18, turn.

**Row 3:** Purl to end; do not cut B but join in C.

**Row 4:** Knit.

**Row 5:** P21, turn.

**Row 6:** K14, turn.

**Row 7:** Purl to end; cut C.

**Row 8:** Using B, knit.

**Row 9:** P23, turn.

**Row 10:** K18, turn.

**Row 11:** Purl to end.

Cast off.

## Belly

**Note:** mark each end of 14th, 27th and 39th rows, to help position legs when making up.

Using 3.25mm needles and C, cast on 18 sts.

**Row 1:** (K1, sl1, k1, psso) twice, k6, (k2tog, k1) twice (14 sts).

Beg with a purl row, work 37 rows in st st.

**Row 39:** K1, sl1, k1, psso, k8, k2tog, k1 (12 sts).

Beg with a purl row, work 3 rows in st st.

**Row 43:** K1, sl1, k1, psso, k6, k2tog, k1 (10 sts).

Beg with a purl row, work 3 rows in st st.
**Row 47:** K1, sl1, k1, psso, k4, k2tog, k1 (8 sts).
Beg with a purl row, work 19 rows in st st.
**Row 67:** K1, sl1, k1, psso, k2, k2tog, k1 (6 sts).
**Row 68:** Purl.
**Row 69:** K1, sl1, k1, psso, k2tog, k1 (4 sts).
**Row 70:** Purl.
**Row 71:** (K2tog) twice.
Cast off rem 2 sts.

## Front legs (make 2)
Using 3.25mm needles and A, cast on 8 sts.
**Row 1:** Inc1 in each st (16 sts).
Beg with a purl row, work 13 rows in st st.
**Row 15:** K1, sl1, k1, psso, k to last 3 sts, k2tog, k1.
**Row 16:** Purl.
Rep rows 15 and 16 four times (6 sts).
**Row 25:** K1, sl1, k1, psso, k2tog, k1 (4 sts).
**Row 26:** (P2tog) twice.
Cast off rem 2 sts.

## Back legs (make 2)
Using 3.25mm needles and A, cast on 8 sts.
**Row 1:** Inc1 in each st (16 sts).
Beg with a purl row, work 19 rows in st st.
**Row 21:** K1, sl1, k1, psso, k to last 3 sts, k2tog, k1.
**Row 22:** Purl.
Rep rows 21 and 22 four times (6 sts).
**Row 31:** K1, sl1, k1, psso, k2tog, k1 (4 sts).
**Row 32:** (P2tog) twice.
Cast off rem 2 sts.

## Ears (make 2)
Using 3.25mm needles and A, cast on 2 sts.
**Row 1:** (Inc1) twice (4 sts).
**Row 2:** Purl.
**Row 3:** K1, (inc1) twice, k1 (6 sts).
**Row 4:** Purl.
**Row 5:** K3, M1, k3 (7 sts).
Beg with a purl row, work 5 rows in st st; cut A and join in C.
**Row 11:** Knit.
**Row 12:** P2tog, p3, p2tog (5 sts).
Beg with a knit row, work 4 rows in st st.
**Row 17:** K1, sl1, k2tog, psso, k1 (3 sts).
**Row 18:** P3tog; cut yarn and fasten off.

## Tail (make 1)
Using 4mm needles and B and D together (one strand of each), cast on 10 sts.
Beg with a knit row, work 28 rows in st st.
**Row 29:** K2tog, k6, k2tog (8 sts).
Beg with a purl row, work 7 rows in st st.
**Row 37:** K2tog, k4, k2tog (6 sts).
Beg with a purl row, work 7 rows in st st.
Cast off.

# Making up
## Eyes
Insert the eyes and fix them firmly in place. Thread the tapestry needle with a length of C and embroider a ring of chain stitches around each eye.

## Body
Insert the side stripes, one on each side of the body, and stitch in place with mattress stitch. Join the belly to the upper body. To do this, turn the chipmunk inside out and stitch the side seams in backstitch, leaving a small gap in the centre of one of these seams. Turn right sides out and stuff the body and head firmly but take care not to overstuff. Stitch the gap closed.

## Legs
Stitch the side seams on the legs and leave the top (sloping) edges unstitched. Push a little stuffing into each leg, then stitch the top part of each one to the body, using the picture of the finished chipmunk as a guide to positioning.

## Tail and nose
Stitch the two long sides of the tail together, then stitch the cast-on edge to the back of the body. Fold each ear in half so that the white part forms the lining; stitch together then attach to the head, following the line of decreases on the front of the head and using the picture of the finished chipmunk as a guide to positioning. Embroider the nose using B.

**Did you know?**
Chipmunks hibernate in winter but they wake up occasionally to have a snack.

DO MOLES HAVE BIG MOLARS?

Did you know badgers are crafters?
They live in close-knit groups!

Do raccoons make a racket?

Are hedgehogs really greedy?

# Techniques

# Getting started

### Yarns

Most of the animals in this book have been made using double-knitting (US light worsted) yarn, though other yarns have been introduced where necessary to produce certain details – such as the fluffy 'eyelash' yarns used for the Hedgehog and for the tails on the Chipmunk, Squirrels and Rabbit.

Yarn spun from natural fibres – such as wool, alpaca, cashmere and silk – has a natural softness and elasticity, so to make these knitted creatures soft and cuddly, either pure wool, pure alpaca, or blends that combine two or more natural fibres, have been used throughout the book. Where it has been difficult to source natural yarns in suitable colours (for the Hedgehog, Squirrels and Frog), yarns that are a blend of wool and acrylic have been used.

The pattern notes for each project give the actual yarns used and by searching online, it should not be difficult to source the same yarns. Of course, since preparing projects for the book, some yarns may have been discontinued or certain colours may no longer be available, or you may simply wish to make your own choice of yarns. However, if a certain yarn is not available or you decide to substitute your own choice, it is important that you knit a tension sample before proceeding with the pattern so that your woodland creature is the correct size and shape.

### Tension (gauge)

To knit a tension sample, cast on 40 stitches using the needle size stated in the pattern and work in stocking stitch (or the stitch stated in the pattern instructions) until your work measures about 5–5½in (12–14cm); cast off loosely. Lay out the piece of knitting on a flat surface and use a ruler (rather than a tape measure) to count the number of stitches and rows over 4in (10cm). If you have more stitches and rows than the number stated in the pattern, you will need to try again, using larger needles; if you have fewer stitches and rows, use smaller needles.

### Needles

The needle sizes that have been used throughout the book may seem smaller than you might expect, and will in most cases be smaller than the needles recommended on the yarn's ball band. In general, 3.25mm needles have been used with DK yarn; this is because you are aiming to produce a firm, close-knit fabric that will hold its shape and not allow any stuffing to poke through.

Many of the component parts of the creatures have been knitted using two needles but most projects will require you to use double-pointed needles to knit at least a few of the pieces in the round.

techniques

### Other equipment

A tape measure and ruler should be part of your basic knitting kit, as well as a blunt tapestry needle, which is essential for sewing pieces of knitting together and weaving in yarn ends, and a small pair of sharp scissors for snipping yarn.

You will need some stitch holders for storing part-finished components: try to make sure you have a few of these, in different lengths, to accommodate different numbers of stitches, as well as a few ordinary safety pins, which are useful for holding just a few stitches. Safety pins are also useful for pinning pattern pieces together prior to sewing-up, and can be used as stitch markers.

Some patterns require you to mark the ends of certain rows, to help when stitching components together; instead of safety pins, you can buy special stitch markers, made from metal or plastic, or you can simply use a paper clip or a short length of yarn in a contrasting colour.

A row counter is useful for keeping track of how many rows you have knitted, while rubber point protectors can be slipped on to your needle ends to prevent stitches from slipping off when you put your work down. You may also find it necessary to use a needle gauge to measure double-pointed needles. All of these items are available from most yarn shops.

### Following patterns

Before you embark on any project, it is important to check the lists of tools and materials at the start of the pattern and make sure you have all the items you require, then read through the pattern from beginning to end to make sure you understand it. If there are any knitting terms or abbreviations (see page 140) that you are unfamiliar with, check the techniques section to make sure you understand what you need to do.

### Safety

If you are knitting any of these creatures for small children, it is vital that you use safe, clean, new materials. Use your own common sense to guide you. The animals pictured in this book have been stuffed using polyester toy stuffing and plastic safety eyes have been used in most cases. Instead of using safety eyes, you may prefer to embroider the eyes using spare yarn, in which case try not to create long loops of yarn that may trap tiny fingers. The Mole has whiskers made from nylon thread, which is also unsuitable for small children, so should be omitted.

# Knitting techniques

All the diagrams are shown for right-hand knitters; if you are a left-handed knitter, try holding the diagram in front of a mirror to view it the other way round.

## Simple cast-on

This is the main method used throughout the book; some knitters know it as the 'two needle' or 'chain' cast-on.

1 Make a slip knot and place it on the left-hand needle. *Insert the right-hand needle into the back of the loop, behind the left-hand needle, and wrap the yarn around it, as shown in the diagram.

2 Use the right-hand needle to pull the yarn through the first loop, creating a new stitch.

3 Transfer this stitch to the left-hand needle and repeat from * until you have the required number of stitches.

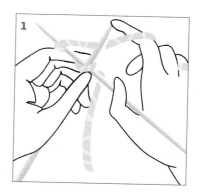

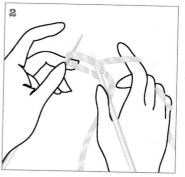

# Cable cast-on

This creates a firm edge and can be used as the initial cast-on method or when casting on extra stitches further on in a pattern.

1 Make a slip knot and place it on the left-hand needle. Make one stitch using the simple cast-on method. *For the next stitch, insert the needle between the two stitches on the left-hand needle.

2 Wrap the yarn round the right-hand needle tip and pull through, between the previous two stitches.

3 Transfer the stitch you have made to the left-hand needle and repeat from * until you have the required number of stitches.

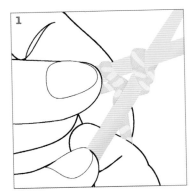

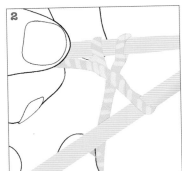

# Knit stitch

Rows of knit stitches produce a garter stitch fabric; alternating rows of knit and purl stitches produce a stocking-stitch fabric – but when knitting in the round, for stocking stitch you use only knit stitches.

These diagrams show work in progress.

1  To make a knit stitch, hold the needle with the stitches in your left hand; insert the tip of the right-hand needle into the first loop, and behind the left-hand needle, and wrap the yarn around it, as shown in the diagram.

2  Use the right-hand needle to pull the yarn towards you, through the first loop, creating a new stitch.

3  Keep this new stitch on the right-hand needle and continue along the row.

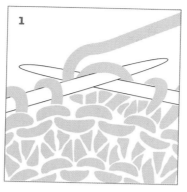

# Purl stitch

These diagrams show work in progress.

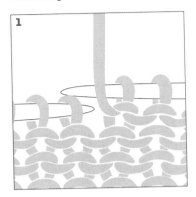

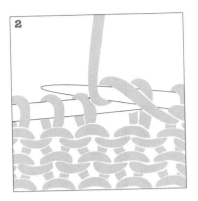

**1** To make a purl stitch, hold the needle with the stitches in your left hand; begin with the yarn at the front of the work.

**2** Insert the tip of the right-hand needle into the front of the next loop, in front of the left-hand needle, and wrap the yarn around it in an anti-clockwise direction.

**3** Use the right-hand needle to pull the yarn through the first loop, creating a new stitch. Keep this new stitch on the right-hand needle and continue along the row.

# Knitted fabrics

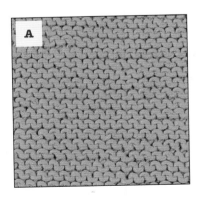

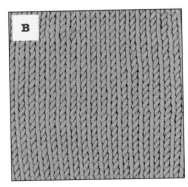

**Garter stitch (A)**
Knit every row.

**Stocking stitch (B)**
Alternate between knit and purl rows.

# Casting off

This is usually done using knit stitches although occasionally you will be required to cast off in purl. To avoid confusion, and make it clear which method to use, the pattern instructions will tell you to cast off 'knitwise' or 'purlwise'.

1 Knit the first two stitches on to the right-hand needle. Then, using the tip of the left-hand needle, slip the first stitch over the second stitch, leaving just one stitch on the right-hand needle.

2 Knit another stitch so that there are two stitches on the right-hand needle, and repeat the process until there is only one stitch left. Cut the yarn and thread the end of the yarn through the remaining stitch to fasten off.

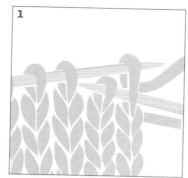

**Did you know?**
Hedgehogs are solitary creatures, only coming together to mate.

# Shaping

### Increases

Increases are worked in one of three ways:

- by casting on extra stitches at the beginning of a row

- by knitting into an existing stitch twice or three times – referred to in the pattern as inc1 or inc2

- by making an extra stitch by picking up the horizontal loop of yarn between the needles, placing it on the left-hand needle and knitting (or purling, where stated) into the back of the stitch – referred to in the pattern as M1.

### Knitting note

Where pattern states 'inc1', knit into the front and back of the stitch, thereby creating one extra stitch. Where the pattern states 'inc2', knit into the front, the back and the front again, creating two extra stitches.

### Decreases

Decreases are worked in a number of different ways:

- **k2tog** Insert the right-hand needle into the front loops of the next two stitches and knit both stitches together.

- **k2tog tbl** Insert the right-hand needle into the back loops of the next two stitches and knit both stitches together.

- **k1, sl1, psso** Slip the next stitch on to the right-hand needle, knit the next stitch, then using the tip of the left-hand needle, slip the slipped stitch over the knitted stitch.

- **p2tog** With the yarn at the front of the work, insert the right-hand needle into the front loops of the next two stitches and purl both stitches together.

- **p3tog** With the yarn at the front of the work, insert the right-hand needle into the front loops of the next three stitches and purl all stitches together.

# Short row shaping

By knitting part of a row, you can create curves and subtle shaping within a piece of knitted fabric. The technique is sometimes referred to as 'turning' or 'turned work' because of the action of knitting a number of stitches, then turning the work and working in the other direction. To prevent creating a hole in the fabric, and to create a smooth transition between stitches, it is advisable to 'wrap' stitches when turning.

1   On a knit row, knit the number of stitches specified in the pattern, then take the yarn to the back of the work, slip the next stitch purlwise from the left-hand to the right-hand needle.

2   Bring the yarn to the front of the work and slip the slipped stitch back on to the left-hand needle; it has now been 'wrapped'.

3   Turn the work so that the wrong side is facing and purl the number of stitches indicated in the pattern. If you are required to turn in a purl row, wrap the stitch by taking the yarn to the back, slipping the next stitch purlwise, then bringing the yarn to the front and slipping the stitch back on to the left-hand needle before proceeding.

4   The action of wrapping stitches will form a series of small bars of yarn on the surface of the work. There is a method of 'hiding' these, where, after a section of short-row shaping has been completed, the bar is knitted together with the wrapped stitch. This method has not been used in these projects, as the bars of yarn tend to create interesting textures in the knitted fabric.

**Note**

In the patterns in this book, to save space, there is no reference made to wrapping stitches. A short row may typically say: 'K21, turn.' This means that, after knitting 21 stitches, and before turning, you will need to wrap the next stitch using the method described here.

*techniques*

**Did you know?**
Foxes belong to the dog family.

# Gathering

You can create shape by gathering. This may be done at the end of a piece of knitting. Instead of casting off, you will be instructed to cut the yarn, leaving a tail, which should be threaded through any remaining stitches. At the making-up stage, gathering stitches are sometimes worked into the fabric – for example, when you are shaping a neck between body and head, or tightening the shape of a muzzle or snout. To do this, stitch a running stitch through the stitches of a single row, using matching yarn, then pull up to the required width or circumference.

Another way of gathering is to run a length of yarn right through a portion of an animal, once it has been stuffed, to create shaping. For some of the creatures – notably the Rabbit, Chipmunk, Badger, Fox and Squirrels – this method is used between the points where the eyes are inserted, either before or after the eyes are fined in place, to help create eye 'sockets' or indentations, and to help ensure that the eyes are positioned towards the sides of the head.

# Knitting in the round

Some of the individual components needed to make up each woodland creature are knitted flat, using two needles, then stitched together to create three-dimensional shapes, while other components are knitted 'in the round' on four needles. Knitting on four needles can be tricky, especially when you are working the first few rows. You will be told to cast on a certain number of stitches, then divide these evenly between three double-pointed needles. To cast on, use the two-needle 'simple' method, which will create a firm, tight edge that is less likely to slip off the needles. All the stitches will be on one of the double-pointed needles, so you will need to transfer the required number of stitches to each of the other two needles and you will use the fourth needle for knitting the stitches.

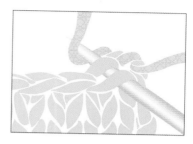

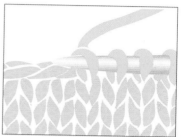

# Picking up stiches

Sometimes the instructions require you to 'pick up and knit' stitches – for example, along the neck edge of the Raccoon. Use the right-hand needle to pick up a loop of yarn between stitches – this may be from the end of a row, or it may be the stitches from a cast-on or cast-off edge – and then wrap the yarn around it and use the right-hand needle to pull the yarn towards you, through the loop, to create a new stitch, just as you do when knitting a row of stitches. Pick up the next loop of yarn to the left and repeat the process until you have picked up the required number of stitches.

# Making up

Making up an animal can be more challenging than knitting the component parts. When creating your woodland creature, whatever its size or shape, the objective is to be as neat as possible because untidy or clumsy sewing will spoil the appearance of your finished project. When joining the sides of two knitted pieces – the row ends – it is advisable to use one of two methods: mattress stitch or backstitch. When joining two straight edges – usually a cast-on edge to a cast-off edge – oversew the edges for a neat result.

Often, in the 'making up' section of a project, you will be instructed to place two component parts 'right sides together' and join them using a backstitch seam, then turn right sides out. If you prefer, or if you find it easier to work with the right sides facing you, you can join pieces using mattress stitch instead.

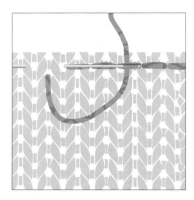

## Backstitch seam

Backstitch seams are usually used to join two side edges of knitting. Even when they are made up of the same number of rows, two edges can be slightly tighter or looser than each other, so to make sure the seam is even, it is a good idea to pin together the edges before stitching.

1 Thread a blunt (tapestry) needle with a long length of matching yarn. Place the two pieces to be joined on top of one another, right sides together.

2 Working from right to left, one stitch in from the selvedge, bring the needle up through both layers then back down through both layers one row to the left.

3 Bring the needle back up through both layers one row to the left, then back down one row to the right, in the same place as before.

4 Repeat, taking the needle two rows to the left each time, and one row back.

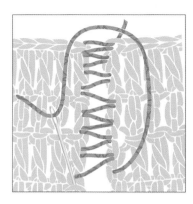

## Mattress-stitch seam

This method creates an invisible seam and is worked from the right side.

1 Thread a blunt needle with a long length of matching yarn. With the right side of the work facing, place the two edges together.

2 Starting at the bottom edge of the work, insert the needle under the bar between the first and second stitches on the right-hand side.

3 Insert the needle in the same way on the opposite edge.

4 Repeat, working across from left to right and back again, moving up the seam. Do not pull stitches tight.

5 When you reach the top of the seam, pull the yarn ends until the two sides meet. Do not pull too tightly or you will cause the seam to pucker. Fasten off yarn ends securely.

## Slipstitch

Using a similar process to mattress stitch, slipstitch (sometimes called ladder stitch or joining stitch) is an almost invisible method of joining the cast-on or cast-off rows of two pieces, or attaching a piece such as a muzzle to the head or legs, or a tail to a body.

1   Thread a blunt (tapestry) needle with a long length of matching yarn (usually the yarn tail left after knitting). Place the piece to be joined in position. Pin in place.

2   Working from right to left, pick up a stitch from the surface to which you are attaching the component, then a stitch a little way in from the edge of the component. Make sure that the needle picks up only one or two threads in each case.

3   Continue in this way, picking up threads alternately from both pieces. Work loosely, so that you can clearly see where to insert the needle. After every six stitches or so, pull up the yarn to tighten the stitches and close up the gap between the two pieces of knitting. Do not pull the yarn too tightly, or you will pucker the fabric.

## Oversewing

Line up the edges to be joined and oversew together on the right side of the work. This method can also be used when applying a piece of knitting on top of another piece (for example, when adding the eye patches to the Pheasant, the stripes on the Badger's head, or the strip down the centre of the Raccoon's face).

techniques

# Finishing touches

There is a bit more to making a knitted animal than simply knitting the component parts and stitching them together. You can subtly alter the angle of a head or the positioning of legs, ears or wings, for example. You'll need to take care over the way you embroider features such as noses.

## Stuffing and stiffening

Take care when stuffing your woodland creature, using plenty of stuffing to create a firm result but not overstuffing so much that you distort the shape or cause excess stuffing to poke through the stitches. For very small components, such as a paw, nose or small ear, instead of using stuffing you could try pushing oddments of yarn inside to add a little extra bulk, including any yarn tails attached to the piece.

For a part of an animal that needs to be more rigid, sometimes filling with polyester stuffing isn't adequate. For the Beaver's tail, for example, which needs to remain quite flat but not floppy, and the Pheasant's tail feathers, which should not droop, cut a piece of craft foam (sometimes called 'funky' foam) slightly smaller than the part to be filled and insert it before attaching the animal part.

## Eyes

Toy safety eyes comprise two parts: the eye, with a ridged shaft, and the washer, which holds the eye in place. Push the shaft of the eye through the fabric, checking that you are happy with the position. Then push the shaft through the hole in the cup-shaped washer on the wrong side of the fabric, following the manufacturer's instructions.

# Embroidery

Thread a blunt (tapestry) needle with a single strand of yarn in the colour required. Insert the needle at an inconspicuous point, such as the nape of the neck, and bring it through the work to the point where you wish to add embroidery stitches, so that the end of the yarn is lost inside the stuffing.

## Straight stitch

As the name implies, this is a single straight stitch. In this book, it is used to create simple details such as a mouth.

## Satin stitch

Use this filling-in stitch for noses and eyes. Bring the needle to one edge of the area you wish to embroider then work straight stitches, close together, to fill in the area.

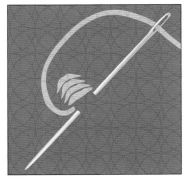

SATIN STITCH

## Chain stitch

This stitch is used to embroider the Bear's mouth and claws and to outline the eyes of the Deer and Chipmunk. Bring the needle up at the point you wish your row of chain stitches to begin. Then reinsert it down through the same point, creating a loop of yarn. Bring the needle back out through the knitted fabric a little way along and inside the loop. Pull the yarn, not too tightly, to create the first chain stitch, then reinsert the needle at the place where it last emerged and repeat to form a row of linked chain stitches.

## Swiss darning

This is a type of embroidery that replicates the knitted stitch; it is sometimes easier than incorporating motifs into the work as you knit. It is used to create patches on the body of the Deer.

If you look at a row of knitting, you will see that each stitch resembles a 'V'. Thread a blunt needle with yarn and bring it up through the point of the V, then take it behind the two prongs of the V and back down into the point, where you began. This stitch is also useful for embroidering a small mouth.

# Conversions

## Knitting needles

| UK: | Metric: | US: |
| --- | --- | --- |
| 14 | 2mm | 0 |
| 13 | 2.25mm | 1 |
| 12 | 2.75mm | 2 |
| 11 | 3mm | – |
| 10 | 3.25mm | 3 |
| – | 3.5mm | 4 |
| 9 | 3.75mm | 5 |
| 8 | 4mm | 6 |
| 7 | 4.5mm | 7 |
| 6 | 5mm | 8 |
| 5 | 5.5mm | 9 |
| 4 | 6mm | 10 |
| 3 | 6.5mm | 10.5 |
| 2 | 7mm | 10.5 |
| 1 | 7.5mm | 11 |
| 0 | 8mm | 11 |
| 00 | 9mm | 13 |
| 000 | 10mm | 15 |

## UK/US yarn weights

| UK: | US: |
| --- | --- |
| 2-ply | Lace |
| 3-ply | Fingering |
| 4-ply | Sport |
| Double knitting (DK) | Light worsted |
| Aran | Fisherman/ worsted |
| Chunky | Bulky |
| Super chunky | Extra bulky |

# Abbreviations

| | |
| --- | --- |
| **beg** | begin(ning) |
| **cm** | centimetre |
| **dec** | decrease |
| **in** | inches |
| **inc** | increase |
| **inc1** | knit into front and back of same stitch |
| **inc2** | knit into front, back and front of stitch |
| **k** | knit |
| **k2tog** | knit 2 together |
| **k2tog tbl** | knit 2 together through back loops |
| **M1** | make a stitch by picking up the loop between stitches and knitting (or purling) into the back of it |
| **p** | purl |
| **psso** | pass slipped stitch over |
| **rem** | remain(ing) |
| **rep** | repeat |
| **RS** | right side |
| **sl1** | slip one stitch |
| **st(s)** | stitch(es) |
| **st st** | stocking stitch |
| **tbl** | through back loop(s) |
| **tog** | together |
| **WS** | wrong side |

# Yarn suppliers

**Artesano Ltd**
Unit G, Lambs Farm Business Park
Basingstoke Road
Swallowfield
Reading
Berkshire
RG7 1PQ
Tel: +44 (0)118 9503350
www.artesanoyarns.co.uk

**Coats Crafts UK**
Green Lane Mill
Holmfirth
West Yorkshire
HD9 2DX
Tel: +44 (0)1484 681881
www.coatscrafts.co.uk

**Cygnet Yarns Ltd**
12–14 Adelaide Street
Bradford
West Yorkshire
BD5 0EF
Tel: +44 (0)1274 743374
www.cygnetyarns.com

**Debbie Bliss**
Designer Yarns Ltd
Unit 8–10
Newbridge Industrial Estate
Pitt Street
Keighley
West Yorkshire
BD21 4PQ
Tel: +44 (0)1535 664222
www.designeryarns.uk.com

**King Cole Ltd**
Merrie Mills
Elliott Street
Silsden
West Yorkshire
BD20 0DE
Tel: +44 (0)1535 650230
www.kingcole.co.uk

**MillaMia UK**
New Kings House
136–144 New Kings Road
London SW6 0AQ
Tel: +44 8450 177474
www.millamia.com

**Rowan Yarns Ltd**
Green Lane Mill
Holmfirth
West Yorkshire
HD9 2DX
Tel: +44 (0)1484 681881
www.knitrowan.com

techniques

## About the author

Having studied Fine Art at the Slade School, Susie Johns began her publishing career as a magazine and partworks editor before becoming a freelance writer and designer. She is the author of more than 30 craft books on a range of subjects including knitting, crochet, papier-mâché and embroidery. She has also contributed to a number of magazines, such as *Let's Knit, Crafts Beautiful, Embroidery, Needlecraft, Woman's Weekly, Family Circle, Practical Parenting* and *Art Attack* and has made several television appearances demonstrating various crafts.

She particularly enjoys doing art and craft activities that involve recycling and reinventing. Susie is a qualified teacher and runs workshops in drawing and painting, knitting and crochet, embroidery, and 3D design. She is the founder member of the East Greenwich knitting group, 'Knitting Night at The Pelton' and an active member of Blackheath Art Society.

Susie has written several books for GMC Publications, including *Knitted Finger Puppets*, *Knitted Pets* and *Baby Booties and Slippers*.

## Acknowledgements

Thanks to Coats Patons, King Cole, Rowan, Artesano, Designer Yarns (Debbie Bliss), Sirdar and Sublime for supplying the yarns used throughout this book. A big thank you to Gerrie Purcell for asking me to do the book in the first place, to Sara Harper for managing the project so patiently, to Cath Senker for editing so meticulously and to Jude Roust for her expertise in pattern-checking. Thanks also to Andrew Perris for photographing the creatures to show them at their best. Finally, a long-lasting thank you to my children for their invaluable patience, support and feedback.

# Index

index

To place an order, or to request a catalogue, contact:
**GMC Publications Ltd**
Castle Place, 166 High Street, Lewes, East Sussex, BN7 1XU
United Kingdom
Tel: +44 (0)1273 488005
www.gmcbooks.com